A HOUSE
FOR HOPE

The Promise of Progressive Religion
for the Twenty-first Century

John A. Buehrens
and Rebecca Ann Parker

BEACON PRESS

BOSTON

Beacon Press
25 Beacon Street
Boston, Massachusetts 02108-2892
www.beacon.org

Beacon Press books
are published under the auspices of
the Unitarian Universalist Association of Congregations.

14   13   12   11   8   7   6   5   4   3   2   1

This book is printed on acid-free paper that meets the uncoated paper
ANSI/NISO specifications for permanence as revised in 1992.

Text design by Wilsted & Taylor Publishing Services

Library of Congress Cataloging-in-Publication Data
Buehrens, John A.
    A house for hope : the promise of progressive religion for the twenty-first
century / John A. Buehrens and Rebecca Ann Parker.
        p. cm.
    ISBN 978-0-8070-0150-9 (paperback : alk. paper) 1. United States—Religion.
2. Liberalism (Religion)—United States—History. I. Parker, Rebecca Ann. II.
Title.
    BL2525.B845 2010
    305.60973—dc22   2009030829

Lines from "Greed," composed by Bernice Johnson Reagon, recorded by Sweet
Honey In The Rock, from *Twenty-Five* (Rykodisc, 1998).

Two lines from "Music Master," in *The Essential Rumi*, translated by Coleman Barks,
reprinted by permission of Coleman Barks.

Dedicated to

the students, faculty,
and staff of Starr King School
for the Ministry,

the members of
the First Parish in
Needham, Massachusetts,

and the memory of

James Luther Adams,
liberal theologian and
prophetic social ethicist

Yes, you have got to assemble
bits of old material.
But into a building.

LUDWIG WITTGENSTEIN,
Culture and Value

Contents

INTRODUCTION

John Buehrens and Rebecca Parker

Hope is rising. The political tide in the United States has turned, and many are hoping for progress on issues such as global warming, health care, marriage equality, and international conflict. But religious fundamentalists of many varieties continue to promote frameworks of meaning that put earth's global community, its diverse peoples, and its ecological systems at profound risk. More than political change is called for; America's liberals and progressives need greater awareness that at the core of social and political issues lie competing responses to the classic questions posed by theology. Effective work for social change requires people of faith who are theologically literate and engaged. To that end, this book provides a primer in progressive theology. It recovers and reconsiders the hope-filled religious frameworks that inspired generations of activists to work for women's rights, racial equality, economic justice, and peace. These frameworks embody reverence for the sacred, nourish community life, carry forward the aspirations of our forebears, and respond to legacies of violence and injustice that harm our bodies and souls. They hold promise for our time. As Sara Robinson, blogging in 2008 for the Campaign for America's Future, argued:

> Secular progressives don't seem to understand that while politics is all about how we're going to make the world better, progressive religion tells us why it's necessary to work for change.... Liberal faith traditions offer the essential metaphors and worldview that everything else derives from—the frames that give our dreams shape and meaning. It has an invaluable role to play in helping our movement set its values and priorities, understand where we are in the larger scheme, and gauge whether we're succeeding or not.
>
> The conservative movement knew from the get-go that it would not succeed unless it could offer people this kind of deeper narrative. Providing that was one of the most important things the religious right brought to their party. Progressivism will not defeat it until we can offer another narrative about what America can and should be—and our liberal churches have longer, harder, better experience than anyone at developing and communicating those stories, and building thriving communities around them.

This book uses the metaphor of a theological house to articulate the "frames that give our dreams shape and meaning." Through this metaphor we explore the classic topics of theology from a progressive vantage point—reminding the reader that liberal religion has a long history, and inviting reconsideration and reimagining of its key concepts. We write as coauthors because we recognize that no one authoritative voice can claim to speak to all of liberal and progressive religion. Dialogue that opens up further conversation is integral to progressive theological method. We have been in dialogue with each other for a number of years about many issues in progressive religion today. We have much in common as a result, but we do not always agree about every issue or formulation. To invite the reader into dialogue as well, in each section of this book there are two or more chapters: one by Rebecca introduces the theological theme and identifies distinctive liberal perspectives on the topic; one by John offers further historical perspective, counterpoints, and reflections on the theme.

Each dimension of the house—including its setting within the natural world—corresponds to one of the classic issues of systematic theological reflection. Theology, we suggest, is architectural—it provides a framework for human life. It is also ecological—it creates an interactive system in response to a specific environment. And it is archeological—it unearths artifacts from the past that can inspire our imagination and understanding now. Here are the basic dimensions and coordinates of this theological house for hope, and the questions that each represents.

I. The Garden

Earth is our habitation—the home that gives us birth and is our final resting place. Building on the liberal theological heritage, which affirms that salvation belongs in this world, how do progressive people of faith regard the earth itself, the reality of death, and the hope for life that is just, abundant, and sustainable for all? Given that earth itself is threatened by global warming, and its ecologies damaged by humanity's failure to establish just and sustainable economic systems, what constitutes a progressive eschatology? Eschatology is the topic in theology that deals with the ultimate "end" of life and of the earth, from the Greek *eschaton*, the last or final things. This is where we begin.

II. The Sheltering Walls

Western society has succumbed to an individualistic set of responses to the gift of life, easily forgetting questions of the common good. Religious community acts to bind us in covenant to one another and to purposes greater than our-selves—not merely as an agreement among mortals but as a shared human response to a sense of grace, interdependency, and responsibility. Put in theological terms, what constitutes a progressive ecclesiology (from the Greek *ekklesia,* which means "gathering together," "assembly," "congregation")? And how can we approach religious community in ways that promote not competitive parochialism but authentic interfaith engagement and cooperation?

III. The Roof

Given the realities of tragedy, oppression, injustice, evil, failure, and sin in the world, what can protect life from harm and repair or restore lives and communities? This is the theological topic of soteriology—from the Greek *soteria,* which means salvation, deliverance, preservation, or release. Religion, at its best, provides shelter for people and communities in need of healing, transformation, or sustenance in difficulty. How might the Bible contribute to the struggle for "deliverance from evil?" What constitutes progressive religion's understanding of what we need to be saved from—and how?

IV. The Foundations

What about God? How can we, or do we, speak of the ultimate mystery that is the source and sustenance of our lives—the source that some call God? Who or what do we most deeply trust? What do we rely on as the foundational given, in relationship to which our lives find their meaning, purpose, and hope? The philosophical foundations of religion have changed over the past two hundred years. Here in America in the early-twenty-first century, a progressive doctrine of God—a theology per se, from *theo*, God, and *logos*, word—must speak adequately both of ultimate reality as creative process and of the hope for liberation and wholeness of all God's children, not in the next life, but in the midst of earthly existence.

V. The Welcoming Rooms

How do we understand not only the nature of God but the nature of our being human together? In the liberal heritage, the notion that humanity is created in the image of God is foundational, making reflection on human experience a primary source of theology, and setting ethics and spiritual practice in the context of an affirmation of human powers and capacities. How do we use our powers for good—including our capacity for sexual intimacy and pleasure, our economic productivity, and our capacity to love, to forgive, and to live as interconnected beings? How do we honor our limitations and need for one another, as well as respect our power and strength? What ideas of relationality, cocreativity with God, agency, and self-transcendence can promote a valid, contemporary form of theological anthropology—a religious understanding of the meaning of being human?

Despite the secular hope that religion might simply vanish, humans continue to be religion-making beings. Within any house of hope, of whatever tradition, there breathes a sense of the Holy, a response to the Sacred Spirit or Spirits present in life, inspiring creativity, compassion, and social action. Worship, art, ritual, and music shape religious community, infusing the atmosphere of its environment, making space for people to breathe. How might liberal religion reclaim a doctrine of the Spirit—a pneumatology (from the Greek *pneuma*, "breath" or "wind")—that affirms the importance of ritual and art?

VI. The Threshold

Finally, without pretending to any messianic powers, what is the mission of a liberal or progressive religious community? If it is not to bring others into one's house to convert them to one's own way of thinking, how can dialogue and partnership with others advance efforts to promote justice and compassion in this world? What constitutes a progressive missiology today—one that offers an open door to hospitable interchanges as essential to the flourishing of life? What thresholds do we need to cross to establish peace? The word "missiology" is from the same root as missive and message—the calling to bring something to others, to the world—and to receive, as well, what others bring to us.

We write in a time of hope—hope that the tragedies of torture and war might be eased, that threats to the earth's environment might be turned around, that economic systems might be converted to better support all earth's peoples and cultures. We also write with the awareness that hope began before we were born. It began with generations of people who lived before us and devoted their lives to what they hoped for their children and grandchildren. We have benefited from their labors, and we take up the tasks of our own time, indebted to them for what has been accomplished and mindful of new challenges, as well as perennial ones that remain. Hope will go on after us, through those who will continue the struggles for justice, equity, and compassion, and will form and reform communities that embody love for life.

"In a house that becomes a home," Antoine de St.-Exupéry writes, "one hands down and another takes up the heritage of mind and heart.... It is needful to transmit the passwords from generation to generation." Such transmission does not always happen. In every generation, rediscovery is needed if the thread of hope is to remain strong. Such rediscovery began for Amy

Moses-Lagos at a protest rally. She was at Fort Benning, Georgia, on a weekend before Thanksgiving, along with thousands of others. They were pushing to close the Western Hemisphere Institute for Security Cooperation, previously known as the School of the Americas. For decades, graduates of this U.S. Army school have been implicated in human rights violations in many parts of Latin America—including torture, assassinations, and mass murder. Amy joined the solemn procession of protesters. Some were shrouded in black, wearing white death masks and shouldering symbolic coffins—full-sized ones in memory of the adults and small ones for the children. Others—including Amy—carried crosses bearing the names of those killed or "disappeared." As they moved, the names of victims of the School of the Americas were read aloud.

"Mirna Chicas," the speaker called. "*Presente!*"—meaning "she is here"—the chorus of protestors responded. The call-and-response continued for hours before the long list of names was completed. "María del Carmen Idarrago de Gómez ... *Presente!* ... Ignacio Ellacuria ... *Presente!* ... Cristino Amaya Claros ... *Presente!* ... Oscar Romero ... *Presente!*" Torture had crucified thousands, but the ritual countered the power of death to obliterate the lost. The protesting community embodied their resurrection, following a practice used in Catholic masses in Latin America that invokes the presence of the dead when the community gathers to break bread and share wine.

"I had never participated in anything like this before," Amy said. "The ritual made me realize that my liberal religious upbringing had taught me to work for social justice, but it hadn't connected activism to theology, to spiritual practice, or to ritual." The ache of a strange absence—a blank theological mind—disturbed Amy. "I wanted to discover whether my liberal religious heritage could offer such grounding," she resolved.

Amy's longing for a religious foundation to her activism brought her to seminary, searching for origins, for identity, and for spiritual sustenance. She knew seminary would be a seed-bed that tended the sources she was missing, a place to return to roots and from which to make a beginning. At Starr King School for the Ministry, Amy told the story of her experience at the School of the Americas' protest, in a class taught by one of us. As president of the school and professor of theology, Rebecca has worked for nearly twenty years with students searching for renewed grounding in theology, spiritual practice, and religious community. She has learned from their struggles and been moved by their discoveries and subsequent activism.

This book is for Amy Moses-Lagos and for readers like her: people committed to resisting injustice and acting in hope, but unaware of the theological perspectives that support their activism or missing a spiritual practice and structure that holds their hope. In response to concerns like Amy's, Rebecca developed the metaphor we use in this book—theology as a habitation. First introduced in a series of lectures for the Liberal Religious Educator's Association and then developed into a popular course, the image conveys that "theology"—whatever else it may connote—is about the structures of meaning that shelter and shape our way of living. The image counters the common notion among liberals that every person must build his or her own theology from scratch—as if religion were only a private matter of personal belief, without history or community. In fact, liberal and progressive people of faith inherit a communal theological house, built by those who lived, labored, and loved before us. Rebecca knows this firsthand; her family heritage includes four generations of liberal Christian ministers and progressive churchwomen. Her friend and colleague John grew up as a Roman Catholic in the Midwest. After leading liberal congregations in Tennessee, Texas, and New York City, and serving as president of the Unitarian Universalist Association for eight years, he is now minister of the First Parish in Needham, Massachusetts, a congregation first gathered in 1711. At Andover Newton Theological School, John has taught a course based on Rebecca's ideas. Both of us have long been engaged in interdenominational and interfaith cooperation—praying, hoping, and working for justice and peace; we are keenly aware of how often people motivated to lives of service are missing an adequate framework for their commitments—one that moves beyond rhetoric, platitudes, and isolated individualism into a sphere of deeper spirituality and shared life with others.

Amy's search is not unlike that of many. A similar struggle with an absence of spiritual grounding troubled the young Barack Obama as a community organizer in Chicago after college. In his early memoir, *Dreams from My Father*, written before he'd ever run for public office, he traces his own uneasy journey to ground his activism in something other than despair and outrage, something abiding and shared, that would alter his sense of an isolated and transient existence. Obama and Amy both reflect a postmodern struggle to regain access to spiritual roots that modernity, mobility, and higher education, with its important commitments to critical analysis, have in one way or another disrupted.

Obama found religious grounding at Trinity United Church of Christ in Chicago, a progressive congregation centered in African American spirituality, theology, and worship. Listening to Dr. Jeremiah Wright preach about "the audacity of hope," he had an awakening.

> In that single note—hope!—I heard something else....I imagined the stories of ordinary black people merging with the stories of David and Goliath, Moses and Pharaoh, the

Christians in the lion's den, Ezekiel's field of dry bones. Those stories—of survival, and freedom, and hope—became our story, my story; the blood that had spilled was our blood, the tears our tears; until this black church, on this bright day, seemed once more a vessel carrying the story of a people into future generations and into a larger world.

Another narrative of rediscovered religious roots and a wider hope is told by Eboo Patel in his book *Acts of Faith: The Story of an American Muslim*. He describes being adrift in the currents of assimilation to the dominant white society that surrounded him as a young Muslim American. Finding inspiration in the social activism of Dorothy Day, Martin Luther King Jr., and Gandhi, he struggled for identity and meaning to match theirs. Gradually, he came to recognize that his Islamic heritage offered him a rich and sustaining religious practice. He embraced his own roots with a transformed understanding of their value and values, while remaining pluralistic in his outlook and interactions. In *Acts of Faith*, Patel demonstrates that interfaith social action can enable people simultaneously to build community with those different from themselves and deepen their grounding in a particular religious heritage.

Our shared hope in this book is that, by reintroducing people to the forgotten theological resources of progressive religion in North America, readers will gain some of the resources that a seminary education can provide and will strengthen their social activism by becoming more firmly rooted in community, ritual, and faith.

It is often forgotten that religion in America has more often than not been liberal in its spirit and progressive in its social impact. The United States was born in an era of Enlightenment religion and increasing concern about human rights. During the early nineteenth century, religious people were at the center of efforts to redress the wrongs of slavery and establish equal rights for women. After the Civil War, and in reaction to the Gilded Age of economic inequality created by rapid industrialization, the reforms of the Progressive Era were inspired in no small part by the Christian Social Gospel movement. Franklin Roosevelt's development of a social safety net in the midst of fighting the Depression, while opposing totalitarianism, found broad religious support in public theologians like Reinhold Niebuhr. In the 1950s and '60s, Martin Luther King Jr., a progressive Baptist, drew on, critiqued, and applied the liberal theological heritage to galvanize the civil rights movement, which found its strongest support among religious people, both people of color and whites, both Christians and Jews. And there has long been far more religious support in America for peacemaking, for lesbian and gay rights, for environmental stewardship, and for women's rights than is often recognized. Few remember, for example, that *Roe v. Wade*, which established abortion as a legal option for women, came to the Supreme Court through the activism of liberal churchwomen.

For nearly three decades now, however, politics and media in the United States have focused on the Religious Right. Starting with the Moral Majority (which never was either) and, later, the Christian Coalition, religious social conservatives have attempted to speak for all of America's diverse religious people. They have been aided and abetted in this by politicians and pundits. The secular media have often found it convenient to frame issues as conflicts between religious conservatives on the one hand and secular individualists on the other. What disappears in such debates is the vast majority of America's diverse people of faith who are not fundamentalists and who care deeply about the common good.

Admittedly, the old mainline and liberal Protestant establishment in America has been in some disarray and has lost the cultural dominance it enjoyed in the 1950s. The liberation and antiwar movements of the 1960s were advanced by many Christians but resisted by others. Unresolved divisions weakened the voice of mainline Protestantism on social issues related to race, gender, sexual orientation, and peacemaking. American Catholicism became divided between the Vatican II–inspired hopes of many laity, religious women, and some priests, and an increasingly defensive stance on the part of the hierarchy. Changes in immigration policy, cultural globalization, the growth of Islam among African Americans and through immigration, and Western interest in Eastern religious traditions have transformed the dominant culture of America to be no longer just Protestant, Catholic, Jewish, and secular but diverse enough to include significant Hindu, Buddhist, and Muslim populations.

Right-wing forces, with divisive political motivations, have eagerly exploited such tensions within the U.S. religious culture. The same reactionary millionaires who funded the conservative wing of the Republican Party funded organizations with such benign-sounding names as the Institute on Religion and Democracy. The IRD then funded many conservative groups within the mainline denominations. The clear goal was to intimidate, distract, and silence the more progressive and prophetic leaders within American religion so that only religious conservatives would be heard. It worked to a distressing degree: the light of progressive religion has been in some eclipse. Within the U.S. Episcopal Church, for example, an investigation by the Diocese of Washington called "Following the Money" found that half a dozen conservative foundations with political agendas were important sources of funding not only for the conservative breakaway Anglican groups within the United States but also for many of the African Anglican bishops they persuaded to help foment theological division. In many instances, the tactics of these conservative groups—

attempting to tag anyone of even moderate religious views as "pro-communist," or as "advancing the homosexual agenda"— have amounted to a kind of religious McCarthyism.

In reaction, many liberal people of faith moved away from religious language and religious frameworks to advance their social justice hopes, forgetting that those hopes had their origins in the ethical teachings of own their religious traditions. This progressive abandonment of religious language and, often with it, religious ritual contributed to the loss of foundations that Amy experienced while retaining a strong social conscience. But recent reaction to the Religious Right is only a part of the story. The liberal religious home and church in which Amy was raised began to erode its own foundations long ago. It introduced important reforms, but in the process it emphasized individual dissent over community building, the primacy of reason over the importance of relationships, and progress toward an idealized future over stewardship of its own heritage.

Amy's religious forebears were liberal Christians, descendants of New England Puritanism who became Unitarians. Beginning in the nineteenth century, many thoughtful Christians—Unitarians among them—began to reject literal interpretations of the Bible as incompatible with science, history, reason, and their ethical sensibilities. They abandoned literal readings of the Bible when they found them to be an insult to reason. They let go of dogmas that didn't make rational sense—such as the Virgin Birth and other miraculous, supernatural acts of God; they critiqued views of God that sanction unjust social arrangements—such as the paternalistic old white man in the clouds who reinforces male dominance. They dissented from notions of God as a controlling and wrathful deity who demands obedience, threatening them with eternal torments or seducing them with heavenly blessings if they obey his will, freeing themselves from being condemned to eternal torment for dancing or playing cards. They questioned exclusivist claims that Christianity was the one and only true religion. They rejected the idea that Jesus's execution atoned for humanity's sins, requiring nothing more of us.

Liberals offered soul-stirring and life-giving alternative theological affirmations in place of the theological stances and pieties they rejected. They placed religion on new foundations: reason, experience, and ethical insight. But too often they taught their children to turn their sights to the new, as if salvation could exclusively be found by leaving the past behind. As a result, their life-giving theological alternatives are what have now largely been forgotten. This book aims to recover those affirmations, update them, and then build on them with a fresh design for the house for hope that is needed in our time.

This book, like our experience as its authors, is rooted in particular streams of religious tradition that are deeply implicated in progressive social movements in America: liberal Christianity and Unitarian Universalism. The latter embraces multireligious life and learning found at the intersections of Islam, Judaism, Christianity, Buddhism, and other sources of spirituality. We share our reflections on these particular traditions as a gift, not a limit. Following the lead of Eboo Patel, we affirm religious pluralism, collaboration, and interchange while simultaneously being grounded in our particular heritages of faith and practice. We seek to extend the welcome and the resources of progressive theology to people who are searching for a religious home that can support their aspirations for a just and sustainable world. At the same time, we are grateful for the opportunity to be guests at the tables of religious fellowship with others and to join with them in mutual learning and transformation.

Hope rises. It rises from the heart of life, here and now,

beating with joy and sorrow. Hope longs. It longs for good to be affirmed, for justice and love to prevail, for suffering to be alleviated, and for life to flourish in peace. Hope remembers the dreams of those who have gone before and reaches for connection with them across the boundary of death. Hope acts—to bless, to protest, and to repair. Hope can be disappointed, especially when it is individual rather than shared, or when—even as shared aspiration—it encounters entrenched opposition. To thrive, hope requires a home, a sustaining structure of community, meaning, and ritual. Only with such a habitation can hope manifest the spiritual stamina it needs to confront evil, endure through trouble, and "hold fast to that which is good."

A renewal of progressive religion is under way in the United States—arising from many quarters. May this volume inspire religious communities in which hope abides, nourished by the Communion of Saints and made strong by theologies that embrace this world in love and struggle.

PART ONE

The Garden

CHAPTER ONE

This Holy Ground

Rebecca Parker

Let us begin with the garden—an image of hope. A lovely Pure Land Buddhist temple that I retreat to from time to time sits among acres of forest, fields, and gardens. Colorful peacocks roam the grounds, which are a living symbol of the Pure Land, the home of the bodhisattvas and the hoped-for spiritual destination of those who chant the name of Amida Buddha. The Christian Bible itself opens and closes with a garden. Genesis pictures God, at the start, planting a garden to be humanity's home along with all earth's creatures and plants. Revelation— the last book of the Bible—envisions God's promised future as a verdant city. A river runs through its heart, and trees of life shelter the city, making it an abode of healing, abundance, and peace. In this alluring vision, human civilization and the paradise garden are united into one community of life. Many houses of worship—from Muslim mosques to New England churches on the green to Buddhist monasteries—would be incomplete without their surrounding grounds and gardens. In a mosque courtyard, you will find flowing water, an elemental symbol of the garden of paradise; just as in the entrance to a Catholic church you will encounter a basin or fountain of holy water, a touch of the healing and saving waters of paradise.

Eschatology, from the Greek *eschatos* (last) and *logos* (word), is the theological term for "speaking of final things"—ultimate hopes. "Where are we going?" "What is the purpose of existence?" "What is the horizon to which our lives are oriented?" All frameworks of meaning involve a perspective on where it all began and where it will all end. "We are dust, and to dust we shall return," the Christian burial service says. We travel "from the Garden to the Garden," suggests Persian poet Jalāl ad-Dīn ar-Rūmī.

Popular forms of Christian eschatology abound. They teach that in the beginning, humanity was created in the image of God to know and love God. In the end, humanity will "meet its Maker" who will judge whom to reward with eternal bliss in heaven and whom to condemn to eternal torment in hell. That's the destiny of our individual lives—and hope for heaven should guide our actions here on earth. The end of the world will come in a cosmic battle of good and evil—Armageddon—in which God's army, led by Christ, will destroy all evildoers and ravage the earth. Following the divine annihilation of this world, God will rescue the true believers—those who have confessed and been faithful to Christ. They will be raptured into the "new heaven and new earth." In this theology, paradise was there at the beginning; humanity was banished from it because Adam and Eve disobeyed God's rules. Their rebellion made this earth into a fallen realm of sin and evil, a place of struggle and suffering, where only fragments of goodness remain. For those who are worthy, paradise will be regained after death or at the end of time. One's best hope is to be among the elect who will be saved in the end.

Such eschatology has powerful social implications. In the

summer of 2006, when war broke out between Israel and Lebanon, news sources reported Christian groups praying for the war to escalate. Christian Zionists hailed the intensification of fighting in the Middle East as a portent that Armageddon was drawing near. Their prayers were based on the sixteenth chapter of Revelation, which forecasts divine acts of violence against earth's seas, river, fountains, air, and sun before the final overthrow of the ruling empire and God's triumph in the battle between good and evil.

Scripts about the end of the world tend to become compulsive, self-fulfilling prophecies. They feed what theologian Catherine Keller calls the West's "apocalyptic habit," the predilection to see the impending end of history in one's own time and to act it out. Mesmerized by stark, apocalyptic either/or choices in a complex world, people drive toward solutions that place hope in destruction. Such theologies imagine that the promise of a new heaven and a new earth—a new paradise garden with its river and trees of life—will arrive in a future on the other side of apocalypse. In the meantime, they bless war and offer no resistance to environmental abuses. Journalist and commentator Bill Moyers notes that "people under the spell of such potent prophecies" represent a significant voting bloc in U.S. politics. As one leading U.S. senator aligned with this theological perspective put it, people cannot be expected "to worry about the environment. Why care about the earth when the droughts, floods, famine and pestilence brought by ecological collapse are signs of the apocalypse foretold in the Bible?"

Variations on this eschatology can be found even in the work of some religious scholars. Popular versions capture the interest of millions of people, as evidenced by books such as the Left Behind novels. If all you know of Christianity comes from these sources, or from what is preached by televangelists, you would have reason to believe this is what Christians in all times and all places have believed—that this is true, biblical Christianity. But this is not so. Progressive people of faith have critiqued this version of Christianity and have created positive alternatives. In our work *Saving Paradise: How Christianity Traded Love of This World for Crucifixion and Empire*, Rita Nakashima Brock and I recover a different vision that flourished in Christianity's first thousand years, before the rise of Crucifixion theologies began presenting Christ as the atoning victim and eschatological judge of humanity's sins. There are also Muslim and Jewish traditions that teach another way.

Progressive eschatologies come in three major forms, all of which move earthward. They hope for the recognition and realization of paradise on earth, rather than after death or after the end of this world. For handy reference, these three alternatives can be identified as Social Gospel eschatology, universalist eschatology, and radically realized eschatology. Each can be captured in a sentence: "We are here to build the kingdom of God on earth," "God intends all souls to be saved," and "Paradise is here and now."

Social Gospel eschatology is the form I know most intimately. I was raised by wonderful Social Gospel Christians. My parents, grandparents, and extended family were church people and ministers. Church was the center of our lives, and even as a young child I understood what it meant to live with purpose. We were here to make God's dream of justice, abundance, and peace real on earth, for all people. That vision was articulated by the prophets in the Bible and reiterated by Jesus. "Let justice roll down like waters!" Amos cries, confronting the warmongers and economic elite of his time who trampled the poor. "Give your bread to the hungry, open your home to the poor, do justice in the market place....Then your light will shine. You will be like a watered garden whose springs never fail," Isaiah promised. As Jesus's followers, our purpose was to work for social change that would "bring in the kingdom." When I was a child, the Social Gospel meant that we as faithful Christians campaigned for integrated, nonrestricted neighborhoods to counteract racism in our community, marched for civil rights, and worked to end the war in Vietnam and advance economic self-determination for people around the world. In the decades that followed, the social agenda for people of progressive faith continued to expand. We advocated for women's reproductive freedom and gay rights; worked for a freeze on the proliferation of nuclear arms; tackled Central American issues; and mobilized to help contain AIDS-HIV and ecological crises.

The Social Gospel vision began at the end of the nineteenth century. Its most prominent leader was Walter Rauschenbusch. A Baptist minister, Rauschenbusch deplored the idea that the purpose of one's life was to escape hell and gain heaven by "taking Christ as our personal Lord and Savior." He thought such a focus on the afterlife was not in keeping with Jesus's attention to life in this world, and he thought it was selfish to be so narrowly concerned with one's own fate when life is social, sustained by an interdependent commonwealth. Rauschenbusch interpreted Jesus's teachings about the kingdom of God—or the "Commonwealth of God," as he preferred to translate the biblical terms—as a vision for life as God intended it to be. Such a vision called people of faith to become coworkers with God to "bring in the kingdom," to fulfill the prayer, "Thy will be done on earth as it is in heaven." He replaced the eschatological vision of a cosmic battle between good and evil with a vision of the struggle we all must engage in this life. He inspired several generations of Christians to work toward making God's commonwealth of justice, abundance, and peace a reality in this world.

Significantly influenced by Rauschenbusch, Martin Luther

King Jr. articulated progressive eschatological hopes in a way that galvanized the civil rights and antiwar movements in the 1960s. The Dream, the Mountaintop, the Promised Land, the Beloved Community—the images King used and the concepts he advanced—made Christian faith into a this-worldly struggle for justice and love, fueled by trust that God's divine purposes are at work in history to bring about the kingdom of heaven on earth.

Immersed in this tradition of Christianity, I learned first-hand its strengths and limitations. Social Gospel Christianity locates paradise in the ideal of what could be, of what God dreams, as voiced by the prophets: liberation of the oppressed, food for the hungry, peace for all people, and reverence for the earth. These are exalted and exalting hopes. I believe in them. At the same time, I know that when their chief habitation is in the divine imagination, as hope for a future toward which we are impelled to strive, all of life is lived in the tension between what is and what could be. The hoped-for future perpetually condemns the present. Now is never enough. The failure of the world to conform to God's vision of justice and abundance is laid at humanity's feet: we have not yet worked smart enough, been well-enough organized, convinced enough people, or corrected the flaws in our approach. Striving to realize "the dream" can be exhilarating, but it can seem to create a spiritual hole that can never be filled and to demand hard work that can never stop. To take a break, indulge in rest, is apostasy. To enjoy life and take pleasure for a moment is at best an indulgence and at worst a moral failing. If God has no hands but our hands, then our blistered, bleeding, and exhausted fingers will have to do. But what do we do when we realize that working with all our might and determination, our strength, is not enough? The mountains of injustice are too high for us to climb. We falter in spiritual exhaustion.

Social Gospel Christianity has had a home in the heart of mainline Protestantism. But mainline Protestantism is now in decline. It is a great vision, but perhaps it has flagged in zeal because weary spirits have labored for an ideal world but have neglected to attend to their own soul's thirst. In the absence of a divine wellspring in the present, when the going gets tough, there is nothing to fall back on. *Ideals* do not administer spiritual assistance; they do not come to the kitchen table in the night of fear when the house has been firebombed. *Ideals* do not surround the soul with comfort or refreshment and renew the heart's courage. For this, something tangible and alive is needed. Something present now.

Universalist eschatology shares much with Social Gospel eschatology. I've come to know its spirit by working among Unitarian Universalists who have inherited this theological tradition. Universalists hope for the earthly realization of God's dream, but they get there by a slightly different theological route: their path responds to the ultimate inclusiveness of God's love. "We are all going to end up together in heaven, so we might as well start learning to get along now," the contemporary Universalist minister Gordon McKeeman explains.

Beginning in early-nineteenth-century America, some Christians argued that fear of hell and hope of heaven do not make for an adequate religion. They saw the debilitating fear created by evangelistic preaching of the type Jonathan Edwards made famous in his sermon "Sinners in the Hands of an Angry God." Elizabeth Cady Stanton, exposed to such preaching as a child, describes creeping out of bed at night, sitting on the stairs, shivering, seeking comfort by the glow of the lights in the parlor, because she was so frightened that the devil would come that night and take her off to hell. Late in life, she wrote, "The memory of my own suffering has prevented me from ever shadowing one young soul with the nonsense and terror of the old theologies."

The universalist Christians preached instead that God's ultimate purpose is the salvation of *all souls.* Hell was not a postmortem realm—it is present in this world when greed, violence, and exploitation wreak havoc on human well-being and the earth. Universalists believed sinners would be held to account for the harm they caused, but that harm had to be redressed here and now, and God's love had the power to ultimately transform all injustice and purify even the most sinful soul, even if it took most of eternity to do so! Heaven could be found in this world wherever love prevails and the gifts of life are stewarded with reverence and respect. And celestial, eternal heaven is where God's love ultimately will transform all humanity.

The universalist perspective on hope is shared by a variety of Christians. Among its earliest proponents was the second-century Christian scholar Origen. Some leading orthodox believers, such as Karl Barth in the twentieth century, have also been universalists. Their hope places profound confidence in the power of God to redeem suffering and injustice, beginning now in concert with human efforts and culminating in eternity.

Universalists critiqued the idea of an ultimate division of the saved and the damned not only on theological grounds but also for its dangerous social implications. They saw that such theology functions to sanction the separation of humanity into those who deserve a larger share of wealth and those justifiably condemned to poverty. It makes the earthly destruction of "evildoers"—those deemed to be the enemies of Christians— into a form of serving God. In the early nineteenth century, the universalist preacher Hosea Ballou noted that if people imagine a divisive and punishing God whose desire for justice is satisfied by the crucifixion of his own son, they will model themselves after this God and feel justified in being cruel themselves. If God terrorizes and condemns sinners, then humans have no obligation to do otherwise. On the other hand, if "God's love embraces the whole human race," as contemporary hymn writer Thomas Mikelson puts it, then here on earth humanity should strive to resolve harmful divisions and conflicts through peaceful means. Based on this theology, many universalists have been pacifists and peace workers.

Many universalists also reject the apocalyptic eschatology that imagines that God will one day destroy the earth. A now obscure universalist book from 1853 by E. E. Guild argued painstakingly on biblical grounds that when the Bible speaks of "the end of the world" it is *not* predicting the divine destruction of the earth. Rather, it is speaking of the end of an age of oppression, an end that arrived with Jesus. Many early Christians believed the "end of the world" referred to the end of the Roman Empire as a power that exploited people and terrorized them with tactics such as crucifixion. The earth itself, God's good creation, is meant to endure as a blessing, not to "melt away." What must melt away are the sins and follies that harm life.

Universalist Christians are not the only ones who emphasize the all-embracing love of God and reject an approach to God based on fear of hell and hope of heaven. Alternative eschatologies can also be found in Islam. A friend and colleague of mine, the Muslim scholar Ibrahim Farajajé, introduced me to the teachings of Rābi'ah al-'Adawīyah, a Sufi Muslim saint, considered to be one of the greatest spiritual authorities of eighth-century Islam. Farajajé tells this story:

> Rābi'ah lived in the city of Basra in Iraq and was said to be consumed with the fire of love and longing for the Beloved, the term of choice for passionate Sufis when referring to the

Divine. One day, she was seen running back and forth across the city carrying a torch in one hand and a bucket of water in the other. When asked what she was doing, she answered that she was going to light a fire in Paradise and pour water on Hell. Why? She said that she was fed up with people basing their relationship with the Divine Beloved on fear of hell or hope of heaven. She wanted to remove both fear of hell and hope for Paradise, for in her perception, both were hindrances to being merged into the Divine Essence.

In reflecting on Rābi'ah, Farajajé notes, "This highly symbolic action calls us to move beyond apparent contradictions, and calls us to remain focused on that Love that transforms, trans-figures, unsettles, disturbs, challenges, makes you think you are losing your mind, comforts, consoles, and liberates."

Radically realized eschatology offers a third way—one that holds promise especially for those who have found idealistic belief in progress too fragile a foundation for sustained social activism. It begins with affirming that we are already standing on holy ground. This earth—and none other—is a garden of beauty, a place of life. Neglecting it for some other imagined better place will be a self-fulfilling prophecy—it will make earth a wasteland. There is no land promised to any of us other than the land already given, the world already here.

If we can recognize this, our religious framework can shift from hope for what could be—for a "better world" to come—to hope that what is good will be treated with justice and love and that what has been harmed will be repaired. This is a different kind of hope. It could be called *responsive* hope, hope grounded in respect for what is here, now. "There are a thousand ways to kneel and kiss the ground," Rūmī wrote. Our framework of meaning can begin with appreciative and compassionate attention to *this* world, rather than imagining an ideal *other* world. Our first prayer can be one of thanks. Instead of striving to get somewhere else, our goal can be to fully arrive here and greet each day of life with gratitude, expressing hospitality for the mysterious goodness that is new every morning and engaging in compassionate care for the present realities of suffering, injury, and injustice that call for our active response.

Western culture's eyes have followed Adam and Eve, clinging to each other, cowering and half-naked, turning their backs on the gates of paradise and wandering into an exiled existence. Those of us shaped by this culture can sometimes feel as lost as they and long to be readmitted to life as it was promised, somehow, somewhere, by someone or something. But what if it is we who have walked away? In our mad dash to get somewhere else, what if it is we who have separated from each other, from the garden, from God calling our name in the cool of the day?

From the perspective of a radically realized eschatology, the problem for Western culture is that we have become disoriented and think we are outside the garden when we are not. We are treating life here and now as if we were in a barren wasteland, but we have profoundly misjudged our location. It is possible to reorient our imagination—as early Christianity did—and to see that the garden is neither closed nor lost but rather is open and present. We can wake from disillusion with a world that poet Matthew Arnold said "seems to live before us as a dream" with "neither life, nor health, nor hope for pain." With Moses, we can see the world lit up from within by the fire of God's spirit and hear a voice calling out to us, "Take off your shoes. The ground on which you stand is holy." We can recognize that the call to resist oppression arises from an epiphany of divine presence in the midst of life's present realities.

"*Today* you will be with me in paradise," Jesus said before he died, and early Christians believed him. Their biblically based eschatology didn't postpone paradise to a distant future; they said Jesus's incarnation and resurrection had reopened the garden, making it accessible here and now. Early Christian sanctuaries, such as those surviving from the fifth century that can still be seen in Ravenna, Italy, were filled with images of the earthly garden of paradise. They sparkle with mosaics depicting green trees, golden dawns and star-lit skies, blue rivers, birds, animals, flowers and fruits. The crucifixion of Jesus was never depicted. Instead, in these landscapes of abundance, the ancestors and departed saints are shown alive. Those revered as martyrs were remembered for how they—like Jesus—held fast to paradise even in the face of trials, betrayals, injustice, and Roman violence. Such faithful witnesses gave evidence that they had tasted and seen paradise. They would not relinquish it—they belonged to life. Along with Jesus, their resurrected presence accompanied early Christian worshippers as they performed rituals training them to taste, to see, and to care for paradise in this world. Baptism symbolically immersed Christian initiates into the waters of paradise, ushering them into a new identity as citizens of paradise. The Eucharist was celebrated as a feast of life. Rooted deeply in these joyous rituals, people gained strength to resist evil, including the evils of imperial domination, exploitation, and persecution.

Irenaeus, a second-century Christian leader, taught that the church has been planted as paradise in this world. The church made paradise tangible by providing help for the needs of bodies and souls and by disrupting social systems that privileged some human beings over others. As a paradise community, the church was countercultural. The powers of life reigned in the church, and its members were to reject the use of violence. The shedding of human blood was a sin. Those who did so violated their citizenship in paradise and needed the healing or retraining of penance to be restored to their place in paradise.

These ancient ways of understanding paradise and of being Christian offer gifts that we can now incorporate into our frameworks of meaning with new appreciation. To say paradise is accessible here and now is not to say the world is perfect or that we should focus on the good and deny the evil and pain around and within us. The serpent lives in the garden, and paradise is a place of struggle, a place where suffering happens and where destructive systems that harm life have to be resisted. But as the early Christian church understood, here is where the hand of comfort can be extended, the deep breath can be taken, and we can live at home in the world, knowing this is enough. A sense of enough is critical now, because anxiety over not enough drives the exploitation and greed that threaten the earth's ecosystems and put cultures and lives at risk around the globe.

Several summers ago, when Rita Brock and I were beginning to work on *Saving Paradise*, we joined my brother's family for a weeklong backpacking trip into the Ansel Adams Wilderness, on the eastern slope of the Sierra Nevada. To get to the trailhead, we took a Forest Service bus from Mammoth Lakes up to Agnew Meadows, and while the bus switchbacked up the narrow road through the pine forest my seat mate struck up a conversation with me. He'd overheard my brother talking with Rita and me about our theological work. He asked if we'd written any books, so I told him about our first book, *Proverbs of Ashes*, which exposes how Christian ideas that the death of Jesus saved humanity have sanctioned domestic violence, sexual abuse, racism, homophobia, and war. He nodded. He said that he had been raised Catholic and that his wife was the daughter of a Methodist minister. Church was important to him.

"I can't believe all the doctrines," he said. "I never was comfortable with the bloody crucifix hanging over the altar—I couldn't understand why we would be worshipping it. But I learned a way of life from the church that I have not rejected."

"What is that way of life?" I asked.

"Oh, it's simple," he said. "Love your neighbor as yourself. Try to help, not harm. Do what you can to make a difference." He went on, "We do foster care for kids." He said it was heartbreaking to see some of the violence, abuse, and deprivation these children have experienced. But he and his wife welcomed them into their home and did what they could. "Not even love can repair the damage sometimes," he said. "I know," I replied.

He asked what book topic I was working on now, and I answered, "Paradise."

"Paradise," he mused, and looked out the window of the bus for a few moments at the bright sky, the deep green pine forests, the alpine meadows coming into view, and, rising above them, the sharp peaks of the Minarets.

"Do you mean 'paradise' like where we are right now?"

"Yes," I said. "Like where we are right now."

We both gazed out the window for a few moments, breathing the pungent fresh air.

"This is enough," he said.

"You know that because you help kids," I said.

A cloud of thoughtfulness passed over his face.

"Yes," he replied, "that's right."

We come to know this world as paradise when our hearts and souls are reborn through the arduous and tender task of living rightly with one another and the earth. Generosity and mutual care are the pathways into knowing that paradise is here and now. This way of living is not utopian. It does not spring from the imagination of a better world, but from a profound embrace of this world. It brings hope home to today, to this moment and its possibilities for faithful love.

Our hope need not be that New Jerusalem will descend

from on high, into the smoking ruins of an earth destroyed by self-fulfilling prophecies of violence. Even less need our hope be that a righteous few will be raptured to another world. Nor do we need to look only to the future, laboring to serve an idealized vision of what *could* be. Our hope can be that from within the heart of *this* world paradise will arise. It will arise from the seeds of Eden sown everywhere; from the life that is within us and around us in our communities and cultures; from the gifts of our resistance, compassion, and creativity; and from the very stones crying out their praise for the presence of God who is here, now, already wiping the tears from our eyes.

CHAPTER TWO

Last Things First

John Buehrens

I walked into her hospital room. Joan was eighty-six. She had both cancer and heart disease. But she was far from ready to go gently into that good night. "You!" she said the minute she saw me. "I've got a bone to pick with you!" She had the church newsletter in her hand. Why, why was there *nothing at all* in it about the most urgent issue of our time—global warming? What kind of religious leader was I, anyway? She went on so adamantly and at such length that, for the first time in more than thirty-five years as a minister, I actually raised my voice to someone lying sick in a hospital bed! "Darn it, Joan!" I sputtered. "You know, it's very hard to be a good minister to you when the first thing you say on seeing me is what a terrible minister you think I am!" She stared at me. "I don't think you're a terrible minister at all. I think you're the best one we've ever had. Which is why I'm *so* disappointed that you aren't saying more about what is so *urgent!*"

A few months later, I told that story at Joan's memorial service. Her friends and family had to laugh. They'd all had similar experiences. Then I added, "Joan was not, shall we say, particularly gifted in the arts of persuasion. She expected me, and all of us, to do the persuasive work—while she provided us a steady stream of news clippings, recipes for a small planet, recycling tips, warnings, and admonitions. Especially near her own end, she spoke with the kind of urgency that has motivated all the great prophets. She didn't want to see the beauty and diversity of this planet squandered. She loved it. And us. Every spring, when the wisteria around her front porch was in stunning bloom, she would tell everyone she ran into to come by to see it, and to enjoy it with her."

Joan raised her children in the atomic age of "duck and cover." She grew old worrying about how much of the earth's beauty would be left for subsequent generations. She might have disdained the idea that she needed a better theology to help articulate and sustain her prophetic vision. But all the great prophets of peace and justice have always begun with a vision of the end, in one way or another. The eighth-century BCE Hebrew prophets warned of a coming "Day of the Lord" when greed, idolatry, and injustice would end, and the meek and humble finally inherit the earth. Early Christians, including the author of the Revelation of John, the last book of the Bible, had not merely an eschatological vision, but also an apocalyptic one—of what would come *after* the destruction of imperial Rome and its oppressions. That vision was expressed in visionary, symbolic terms.

When I was in theological school, at the height of the civil rights, antiwar, and nuclear freeze movements, student lore said that the one question you would almost surely have in your final oral exams was, "What characterizes an authentic prophet?" You could cite various biblical criteria as long as you made it clear you knew that "an authentic prophet always prophesies doom," providing moral warnings before offering any hope to a saved or saving remnant.

No wonder so many progressive people want to avoid a topic like "eschatology" altogether! After all, to be progressive is to hope in, well, *progress* of some kind. Besides, all too often conservative theology has dominated the discussion with a form of eschatology that does little to encourage a responsible relationship to the world that sustains us. During the 1970s the best-selling religious book in America, almost outselling the Bible, was Hal Lindsey's *The Late, Great Planet Earth.* This apocalyptic reading of the then-current "signs of the times," added to tendentious and literalistic readings of the symbols in the books of Daniel and Revelation, led Lindsey to predict that crises in the Middle East would result in U.S.-Soviet nuclear war and the end of all life except for those few believers "saved to eternal life." Progressive theologian Martin Marty aptly reviewed Lindsey's book in a single sentence: "This author gave up on the world before God did."

There are, you see, also false prophets. The usual ratio of false prophets to true, said a teacher of mine, is probably about the same as it was in the time of the prophet Elijah: about 450 to 1. One can prophesy in the name of an idol—believing that some portion of the whole alone is holy. Pundits can prophesy for popularity and profit, insincerely. Even the most faithful and sincere can turn out to be quite wrong, however. "My ways are not your ways," said the Lord to Isaiah.

Fundamentalists have lost such humility when they pretend to use the scriptures as a key to the future. Many have become seduced by an escapist fantasy—when the end does come, and soon, "the saved" will be snatched up bodily in "the Rapture," whereas the rest of us will be left behind. Many of us driving the roads of Bible Belt America have followed bumper stickers reading, "Warning: In Case of Rapture, This Car Will Be Driverless." (Among the numerous parodies, my favorite is one saying, "In Case of Rapture, This Car Will Be Pulled Over, for Driver to Rethink Eschatology.") Once I even had the experience of boarding an airplane in Dallas behind a pilot who was carrying one of the popular Left Behind novels by Tim LaHaye and Jerry Jenkins. Not surprising: there are more than sixty million in print, not counting the eleven million in a children's series. Maybe I'm just envious of their colossal book sales. But as one of my theological mentors put it, "There is nothing quite so salable in America as egotism wrapped in idealism." To which I would add, "And then pandering to widely held fears."

The late Gerald Durrell (brother of the novelist Lawrence Durrell) was a zoologist who had an appropriate fear that in our lifetimes we are betraying our Creator by overseeing the irremediable extinction of many species and so much biodiversity. Before he died, he wrote a letter to be sealed in a time capsule alongside his body. In it he said, in part,

> The world is to us what the Garden of Eden was supposed to be to Adam and Eve. Adam and Eve were banished, but we are banishing ourselves from our Eden. The difference is that Adam and Eve had somewhere else to go. We have nowhere else to go. We hope that by the time you read this you will have at least partially curtailed our reckless greed and stupidity. If we have not, at least some of us have tried.... All we can say is learn from what we have achieved, but above all learn from our mistakes, do not go on endlessly like a squirrel in a wheel committing the same errors hour by hour day by day year after year century after century as we have done up to now. We hope that there will be fireflies and glow-worms at night to guide you and butterflies in hedges and forests to greet you. We hope that there will still be the extraordinary varieties of creatures sharing the land of the planet with you to enchant you.

We *hope.* Progressive eschatology has the courage to hope for justice, peace, and sustainability in *this* world. The one we have been given. Too much conservative religion hopes only for piein-the-sky-by-and-by. Whether there is, or is not, a life after this one, none of us can say for certain. When encouraged toward the end to prepare for the next world, the great naturalist and progressive Henry David Thoreau is said to have replied, "One world at a time." And when asked if he had made his peace with God: "I wasn't aware that we had quarreled." "I may not get there with you," Martin Luther King Jr. said in his final sermon, "but I have been to the mountaintop. I have seen the promised land!" He meant the promise of God's *shalom*, of peace born of justice, fulfilled in this life, not another.

Joan, who talked back to me from her hospital bed, was first cousin to a white ally of Dr. King's—Albert D'Orlando, a leading progressive minister in New Orleans during the civil rights era. Even then she was a member of the congregation I now serve, the First Parish in Needham, Massachusetts. Descended from Russian Jews through her mother and Italian Protestants through her physician father, Joan was a religious rebel. Like Thoreau and King, she had little interest in having a share in any celestial real estate. Heaven for her was basking in the glory of a summer evening looking out at the ocean at the cottage that she and her late husband had inherited on an island off the coast of Maine. It was in the dream of human justice and peace in a sane, sustainable economy. If she fit anywhere among mortals, she fit in best with Unitarian Universalists—descendants of those Puritans and Enlightenment rationalists who in the late 1700s played such a key role in the founding of the American Republic.

First Parish was gathered in Needham in 1711, when some thirty local farmers covenanted to form their own congregation rather than ford the Charles River to go church in nearby Dedham. When New England preachers like Jonathan Edwards led revivals based on fear of future hellfire and damnation, Needham's founding pastor, Jonathan Townsend, was skeptical of such methods. Perhaps he thought them unnecessary. The

Puritans knew about the wisdom of pondering one's mortality. Every gravestone was a *momento mori.* So were their devotions. After all, the meetinghouse sat next to the town burying ground. It was "a serious house on serious earth," as poet Philip Larkin once phrased it, "if only that so many dead lie round." A place, as even the modern scoffer in his poem, "Churchgoing," realizes, is "proper to grow wise in."

Puritan eschatology, however, was one of hope. They hoped for heaven but also for the thousand-year reign of Christ here on earth, the millennium. That would come, they believed, only when the gospel had been spread worldwide, to all the heathens. Their own "errand into the wilderness" was to establish some of God's kingdom here on earth in anticipation of its coming fullness. First by organizing their own lives "in kingdom fashion," and then by converting or eliminating the Native Americans they encountered.

Such a theology led to tragic endings. Native Americans, first devastated by European diseases, were either made Christians ("praying Indians") and their lands seized or purchased on the cheap, or they were subjected to genocidal warfare. The landscape of New England was then deforested—for buildings, fuel, and pastures. To this day, the official seal of the Town of Needham depicts a Puritan purchasing the twenty-five square miles of the original town from the one surviving native—a converted Indian called William Nehoiden (or Nahanton)—for the equivalent of two months' pay for a poor country parson. Today, house lots of one-tenth of an acre in town sell for nearly half a million dollars.

When "progress" came, in the form of railroads, in the mid-nineteenth century—around the same time that they came near to Thoreau's retreat at Walden, about fifteen miles north—entire Needham hills and gravelly sections of land were scooped up and taken by rail to fill in Boston's Back Bay.

The rail lines created two new town centers, in East Needham and West Needham (Wellesley). First Parish was left distant from both, sitting by the old burying ground, out in the middle of nowhere. In 1879 the meetinghouse itself was put up on log rollers and moved by horses to a new foundation near the central railway stop. A new town hall was built across the way; Wellesley became a separate town.

I take this story as a symbol of what nineteenth-century Americans did with eschatology. They tended to see the kingdom of God as gradually being realized right here on earth through their works of human "progress." Never mind that the spreading of settlements and the railways across the middle of the continent also brought with them the slaughter of the great buffalo herds, the confinement of Native Americans to wretched reservations, and the plowing of vast stretches of prairie at enormous environmental cost. Despite criticism by some progressive religious leaders of such developments as the Cherokee removal in the 1830s, the annexation of Texas and the war against Mexico, and the injustice of slavery, the dominant theological-political view was that America was simply fulfilling its God-given "manifest destiny." Surely such material progress would be accompanied by spiritual progress as well.

Nathaniel Hawthorne once satirized this misplaced confidence in an allegory titled "The Celestial Railroad." Based on the Puritans' favorite devotional work, John Bunyan's *Pilgrim's Progress*, this updated pilgrimage is led by a railway director named Mr. Smooth-it-Away. He has bridged over the famous Slough of Despond "by throwing into the Slough some editions of books of morality, volumes of French philosophy and German rationalism, tracts, sermons, and essays of modern clergymen, extracts from Plato, Confucius, and various Hindoo sages, together with a few ingenious commentaries upon texts of Scripture; all of which, by some scientific process, have been converted into a mass like granite. The whole bog might be filled up with a similar matter." Riders find his bridge very shaky, however. There are many other defects and problems. And the railroad never does arrive at its destination, the Celestial City.

What the nineteenth-century myth of progress often did lead to was romantic nostalgia. In *The True and Only Heaven: Progress and Its Critics,* the late historian and social critic Christopher Lasch pointed this out. He took his title from Hawthorne. But even Thoreau, when he explored the woods and rivers of New England, often expressed nostalgia for the vanished Native Americans of the region. Still, he gave courage to some who tried to resist the dominant belief that the kingdom of God could be advanced by proselytizing, by spreading Christian "civilization," and by exploiting both the land and its peoples.

By the end of the nineteenth century, many sensitive religious leaders in America's largest cities were questioning whether laissez-faire capitalism wasn't creating something more like hell on earth than heaven for industrial workers, for freed African Americans, and for new immigrants. They questioned whether evangelism focused on individual conversions was sufficiently faithful; whether something more wasn't required of the privileged by way of creating material and political conditions more likely to support lives of spiritual integrity and of hope. The Social Gospel movement, as it became called, was closely linked to the Progressive era and its reforms.

I once had an older parishioner who was raised very much under the influence of the religious liberalism of that era. She described to me how the Sunday school in which she was raised prominently displayed a five-point statement of religious liberalism that was a clear response to the five points of traditional Calvinism: "The Fatherhood of God, the Brotherhood of Man, the Leadership of Jesus, Salvation by Character," she recited, "and the Progress of Mankind Onward and Upward Forever." Then she added firmly, "But I never quite believed that last one, you know."

She had by then lived through times that had seen the trench warfare of World War I, the hardships of the Great Depression, the rise of totalitarianism, the horrors of the Holocaust and of World War II, and the anxieties of the new nuclear age—among other things. These events forced a great many progressive religious people to have to reconsider whether their eschatology—and even their view of human nature, their theological anthropology—had not proved to be too naively optimistic.

Yet it is easy for the privileged to lapse into what Forrest Church has called "the sin of sophisticated resignation." These lapses keep the privileged from fully facing the spiritual poverty of materialism run amuck, or becoming aware of how great the forces are that hold people—privileged and disadvantaged alike—captive to injustice and evil. The oppressed know better. Toni Morrison, in her novel *Sula*, puts it this way:

> What was taken by outsiders to be slackness, slovenliness, or even generosity was in fact a full recognition of the legitimacy of forces other than good ones. They did not believe doctors could heal—for them, none had ever done so. They did not believe death was accidental—life might be, but death was deliberate. They did not believe Nature was askew—only inconvenient. Plague and drought were as "natural" as springtime. If milk could curdle, God knows robins could fall. The purpose of evil was to survive it and they determined (without ever knowing they had made up their minds to do it) to survive floods, white people, tuberculosis, famine, and ignorance. They knew anger well but not despair, and they didn't stone sinners for the same reason they didn't commit suicide—it was beneath them.

No wonder so many of the most influential and important theologies that have emerged in recent decades have been theologies grounded in the real-world experiences of the poor, the oppressed, and the marginalized. These theologies of liberation are varied, depending upon the experience of different forms of oppression. But they all seem to have this in common: they have variously tried to express what Cornel West has called "the courage to hope." Some of this hope may be for progress toward human rights, democracy, and a more prosperous future. But the strongest forms of it are what Rebecca Parker has called "responsive hope," grounded in gratitude for the gift of life itself.

Surely my parishioner Joan was right: in the face of our shared oppression of the earth itself, there is an urgency. But it must not be one marked by apocalyptic fear. Rather it must be an urgent need to reconstruct and renovate the kind of hope that is at the heart of progressive spirituality. Ecological destruction is interrelated with every social injustice—war, sexism, racism, and poverty. Many wise and reflective evangelicals, after all, are at last beginning to take seriously our responsibility as humans for stewardship of the creation. This in itself is something of a sign of hope. But what is needed is the kind of realistic hope that can make our work together persistent, patient, and persuasive.

Every progressive religious community I have served over the last thirty-five years has tried to do this, by pioneering in recycling, promoting Earth Day celebrations, raising ecological consciousness, organizing to protect the environment. In Needham, we recently renovated the meetinghouse and, despite a modest increase in its physical footprint, cut the building's carbon footprint by almost half. We plan to do more.

Some people think Western religion is all "dominion theology" and a threat to the environment. So postreligious people who think of themselves as liberal and progressive have no difficulty singing, as at Woodstock, Joni Mitchell's lyrics, "We've got to get ourselves back to the garden," or John Lennon's "Imagine"; or resonating with the rhetoric of Martin Luther King Jr. saying "I Have a Dream"; or joining Barack Obama's echo of his former pastor in calling for "the audacity of hope." But without an articulate theology and without communities of spiritual discipline and support, many continue to indulge themselves in unrealistic approaches, easy forms of despair, or an impatience that fails to persuade.

So let us begin where we all hope to end: in gratitude— with a radically realized eschatology. After all, if Jesus was an eschatological preacher, warning contemporaries about the consequences of self-indulgence, injustice, and oppression, he also preached that the kingdom of God is right here among us wherever and whenever we make it real by loving the very ground of our being with all our heart, mind, and strength and by refusing to give our allegiance to any oppressive power. It is among us when we love our neighbors, even the very least of these, as we should also love ourselves. It is among us when we put our anxieties over what to eat, drink, and wear into proper perspective and consider the lilies of the field. For we are in the garden of creation, where surely not even Solomon in all his glory was adorned like one of these. So may our final words, at the end of lives, be words of thanks. And may we sustain all our efforts and hopes along the way in that same spirit.

PART TWO

The Sheltering Walls

CHAPTER THREE

Life Together

Rebecca Parker

Let the walls of our theological house symbolize the shelter of community. "May they be strong to keep hate out and hold love in," Louis Untermeyer implores in his poem "Prayer for This House." Within the embrace of sacred gathering places, people come together to form connections with one another and with that which is holy and life-giving. A religious community's encompassing walls—real or metaphorical—can be portable, as with the ancient Hebrews' tent of meeting, or permeable, as with the Druids' circle of standing stones and the enslaved African Americans' "hush arbor" in the forest. Or they can be as solid and imposing as the buttressed walls of a gothic cathedral. Whatever the character of a community's structures, they function to support the survival and thriving of a people.

There is no life apart from life together. In many Buddhist traditions, taking refuge in the *sangha* (the spiritual community) is necessary for enlightenment. "There is no salvation outside the Church," said third-century Christian bishop Cyprian of Carthage. These may be startling claims if you have been steeped in the dominant U.S. culture of individualism, which suggests that looking out for number one is the only way to survive. But life is relational through and through. Everything exists in interaction and interdependence with everything else. The question is not *whether* we are social, connected beings. That is a given. The question is *how* we shape our modes of being with one another and with the sources that uphold and sustain life.

"Ecclesiology," from the Greek word *ekklesia* (called together), is the theological theme that speaks about religious community. Ecclesiology asks, "What is the nature and purpose of a religious community? What brings the religious community into being and holds it together? How does the community define the relationships and roles of its members? What rituals and spiritual practices align the community with what it understands as the sacred, the source of life?" A classical Christian answer to these questions speaks in metaphors and goes something like this: the church is the living body of Christ and the means by which Christ's gift of salvation is made available to humanity. Its purpose is to incarnate the life of Christ in the world—his ministry of teaching, healing, and liberating the poor and oppressed. The church is brought into being by the grace of God and sustained by the presence of the Spirit. Members of the church are to use their diverse gifts to uphold the community and enable it to fulfill its purpose—they are to be of service to one another and to society. The church's primary rituals are the sacraments of baptism and Eucharist, with their symbols of water, bread, and wine. Through spiritual disciplines such as praying, interpreting scripture, and sharing resources for the common good, the church aligns itself with the sacred source of all life, which is God.

This language is lofty, and the sense of purpose it captures can give profound meaning to life. But the reality of religious community—Christian and otherwise—has not always been a blessing. Our culture has developed a deep distrust of organized religion, often for good reason. The recent scandals of sexual abuse by priests are a reminder of how destructive organized religion can be when it holds young people captive to sanctified structures of authority in which they become easy targets. Oppressive religious community can be soul destroying: the threat of hell for those who do not toe the line, shunning or exclusion for those who stray from the required practices, dominating ideologies that stifle critical thinking and expect people to check their intelligence at the door. Religious communities whose ideas, rituals, and symbols imbue violence with meaning produce genocide, crusades, inquisitions, and terrorist acts.

The perils of religious community have left many liberals and progressives convinced that organized religious communities cannot be trusted; they pose too many dangers and break too many promises. They fail to embody what they profess and disappoint those who invest their lives in them. Such wariness about religious community puts liberals and progressives in sacred company. The Hebrew prophets condemned religion when its priests soothed the privileged but neglected the poor. "I hate and despise your solemn assemblies," God announces in the book of Amos. "Take away the noise of your singing, stop your ritual sacrifices. Instead, let justice roll down like waters!" Jesus overturned the money changers' tables at the Jerusalem Temple, crying, "You have made my father's house into a den of thieves." Protestant Christian reformers of the sixteenth century called the Roman pope the Antichrist. John Calvin, one of the most influential church reformers of all time, pronounced the church to be a house always under reconstruction. Martin Luther nailed his indictments of the Roman church to the doors of Wittenberg Cathedral, protesting religious systems and practices that exploited people.

From the sixteenth century forward, church reformers have sought to correct the abuses of the Western Christian church, beginning by tearing down the old structures. Some reformers physically assaulted churches—shattering images of the crucified Christ and stripping churches of their rich ornamentation. They condemned the unholy alliance between the church, the aristocracy, and the economic elite—all of whom benefited from Crucifixion-centered theologies. In England, radical Puritans agitated for the overthrow of all three to alleviate the hopelessness and suffering of the poor and the imprisoned. Anabaptists—precursors to today's Baptists—and other groups in what scholars call the left wing of the Reformation rebelled against the church's domineering control by eliminating nearly all ritual and hierarchy. No one was to be conscripted into Christ's service against his will—individual free choice and personal responsibility to judge beliefs for oneself based on reading the Bible became the new building materials for religious community.

Radical reformers broke the stained glass out of windows and replaced it with clear glass to admit light by which to read the Bible. Instead of having doctrine dictated to them by priests, bishops, and religious scholars, individuals could read, think, interpret, and decide for themselves. Church was to become a chosen society—not a community that one was born into and gained membership in by inheritance. The right—even the duty—of individuals to break free from the impositions of an unjust religious body became a defining habit of Protestant Christianity.

As a result, liberal and progressive people of faith are often more at home alone than in company with others. The twentieth-century architect Frank Lloyd Wright, who designed a number of Unitarian church buildings, was once asked what he thought of organized religion. His response: "Why organize it!" Many liberals, consciously or not, seem to prefer that their religious institutions remain weak, underfunded, or distracted by endless attention to "process" and checks on the exercise of power. Too much money, power, or organization, it is feared, will lead to corruption. One friend of mine, a progressive United Methodist lay leader and community activist, quips that liberal religion teaches that you can do anything you feel called to as long as you are willing to do it alone.

The ecclesiological questions for progressive people of faith then become these: Is it really preferable (or even possible) to be religious alone? Or, is there an importance to religious community life that needs to be claimed anew, while protecting against the liabilities and dangers that community life can pose? I strongly believe the answer to the first question is no and the answer to the second is yes. We need life together, and liberals would be wise to invest in rebuilding the walls of community. My suspicion is that religious conservatism has grown not because its theology is more inspiring than that of liberal theology, but because conservatives in recent decades have been better at creating and sustaining religious communities that offer people meaningful connection with one another and support in enduring life's trials and tribulations.

The history of progressive ecclesiology is worth reconsidering for the gifts it may offer us now in a new quest for liberal and liberating community life. Two progressive theological claims about congregational life stand out. First, congregations can be "communities of resistance"—countercultural habitations in which people learn ways to survive and thrive that can resist and sometimes even transform an unjust dominant culture. Second, congregations can provide an embodied experience of covenant and commitment among people; they can foster freely chosen and life-sustaining interdependence. A third claim needs renewal and reconstruction, and it will be explored more deeply in chapter 11: congregations can ground life in shared rituals that nourish and strengthen people spiritually, emotionally, psychologically, and intellectually, providing a deep foundation for courageous and meaningful living.

Communities of resistance enable people to collectively resist oppression, something that can rarely be done alone. Many people raised in black churches testify to how their churches functioned as countercultures to white supremacist culture. African American church traditions began in the nineteenth century as critical responses to a white Christianity that used the Bible to enforce the obedience of slaves to their masters. In defiance of such teachings, black leaders—women and men—articulated alternative interpretations and appropriations of the Bible, and they forged life-sustaining worship practices that drew on African spiritual traditions. Following Emancipation, through the church, people whose lives were made hard by an exploitive, dominating culture built ways of life together that promoted their survival and thriving. Education, preaching, and worship, systems of practical care, and activism for social change shaped the lives of church members into meaningful patterns of resistance, dignity, and authority. In her book *Righteous Discontent: The Women's Movement in the Black Baptist Church*, Evelyn Brooks Higginbotham shows how women took the lead in black church organizations, which served as a training ground for wider service:

> These churches have been and still are the great preparatory schools in which the primary lessons of social order, mutual trustfulness and united efforts have been taught.... The meaning of unity of effort for the common good, the development of social sympathies, grew into women's consciousness through the privileges of Church work.

The black church has its flaws and failures, which African American people of faith confront. Heterosexual and patriarchal privilege still hold sway in many black churches, and some new movements are aligned with a prosperity gospel that accommodates itself to consumerist culture. Those black ministers and congregations that struggle with these limits and liabilities embody the spirit that continually challenges and disrupts the captivity of Christianity to an unjust status quo. As Dr. King said, there are some things to which one should never become adjusted. Dissent remains a radical act of faith.

Religious communities of resistance can be found around the world. I traveled a few summers ago to visit Unitarian congregations in Transylvania. Part of the Hungarian minority in Romania, the Unitarian villages are largely found in mountain valleys. They've been there for 450 years. During the Reformation, dissident Christians found refuge in this region from the hunt for heretics, and when the official church cracked down on scientists who were developing new theories about the solar system, the Unitarians maintained a space for reason and science as part of religion.

In Okland, Transylvania, Rev. Levente Kellerman took me into the sanctuary to see the ceiling of the centuries-old Unitarian church in his village. In typical Transylvanian style, the church has a wooden ceiling crisscrossed with beams, creating a latticework of deep squares that are painted with folk-art depictions of flowers and plants. But one square was different: it depicted a golden sun surrounded by circling planets in a star-spangled indigo sky—a diagram of the Copernican solar system.

In visiting with them, I learned that Unitarians, in contrast to all other Christians in their region, perform the rituals of baptism and confirmation in the season that *follows* Easter.

Though their neighbors baptize at Easter in symbolic reenact-ment of the death and resurrection of Jesus, the Unitarians baptize to reenact the period after Jesus was crucified when a handful of his disciples came together and pledged to carry on his teaching and his ministry. For them, to be baptized means to join the community of Jesus's disciples, who in defiance of a crucifying empire persist in the ways of compassion. The motto of their community, taken from Jesus's instruction to his disciples on how to handle themselves in contexts of op-position: "Be wise as serpents and gentle as doves."

In the twentieth century, when the communists came into power in Romania, they imprisoned many of the Unitarian ministers. The dictator Ceausescu launched a plan to systemat-ically destroy the Unitarian villages—flooding some and bull-dozing others. The children born in this time were taught early by their parents to put up an appearance of compliance and cooperation. They joined the Communist Youth and dutifully mouthed the slogans and songs. But as one young Transylva-nian minister, a woman, explained to me, "At the same time that we were going to the Communist Youth meetings we were also participating in a counter-education system, conducted by the church members. After school we would go to various homes—different homes on different days—and the elders would teach us about our religious heritage, our obligation to resist as disciples of Jesus."

Liberation from oppression often depends on the existence of such counter-education systems and communities of resis-tance. The fall of the Ceausescu regime began in December 1989, with an uprising in Temesvár sparked by the arrest of Rev. László Tökeś. A leader of the Calvinist-Reformed Com-munity, Tökeś was an outspoken critic of Ceausescu's project to destroy the rural Hungarian communities in Transylvania. In response to his witness, people took to the streets to demand an end to the totalitarian regime. Their spirit of dissent had been sheltered and nurtured by religious communities. When the time was ripe, they acted to instigate change.

Such community is established less by a historic creed or by apostolic tradition than by covenantal relations among the members. The role and responsibility of the members includes thinking for themselves, exercising their power to interpret scripture, to bless what is holy and to critique what is unjust, in a "priesthood and prophethood of all believers." Diversity and dissent are holy gifts. Rituals and spiritual practices are subjected to ethical criteria: do they support actions that are compassionate and just?

When religious communities are formed by the will of the people themselves and governed by the members, they can be liberating and life-giving places. This is the notion of "covenanted community" that emerged from the Christian reformers of the sixteenth century and was transported to America with the pilgrims and the Puritans. In place of a hierarchical church authorized by tradition and governed by priests, bishops, and popes, they insisted congregations should be organized by people coming together and making a covenant to "walk together" in their spiritual lives. Covenanted religious communities rest on the authority of their members, who have voice and vote in church governance (although, historically, in all but the most radical communities it was only the men who could vote). In place of an established creed that all consented to, people were to consent to the common agreements of the community, worked out through democratic process.

Covenant itself does not assure just and sustainable community. It can foster circles of exclusion that justify harmful treatment of those deemed outsiders. The Puritans who came to New England segregated themselves from those they regarded as outside the covenant, with tragic results for the indigenous people whom they tried to assimilate, to segregate onto reservations, or to annihilate through war. Similarly, in South Africa, Calvinist Protestants, driven by their theology of covenanted community, established a white elite and an apartheid system for blacks and coloreds enforced through violence and suppression.

James Luther Adams advocated covenantal community, but he recognized the necessity of correctives. The covenant itself, he argued, should be directed to the thriving of all beings and all life, not just some. Furthermore, those within the covenant need to hold themselves accountable to something or someone beyond their own group. The community can hold itself accountable to its best interpretation of God's intention for life as revealed in scripture and tradition and through prayer. It can hold itself accountable to those most at risk of harm. It can hold itself accountable to the revelations of science and reason. Different religious communities relate to different transcendent sources, or a combination. With an adequate accountability practice in place, the sheltering walls of community can bless the community's members and also be a blessing to the larger society.

How can people move beyond isolation, a banal individualism, and a lack of purpose? One way is by coming together with others in religious communities that fire our intellects, touch our hearts, connect us in loving support with others, turn us to face the world's painful realities with honesty and critical analysis, and direct us into deeds of service and social activism. Through assembling—coming together—people can harness what James Luther Adams called "the organization of power and the power of organization."

In our time, people are searching for a renewed experience of liberal religious community. I gained insight into this from my cousin Megan. A few years ago, Megan was in a period of personal despair after an unexpected and painful breakup. Her family and friends were worried for her. Then one day, Megan invited me to lunch, bursting with good news.

"I have been born again!" she announced, beaming. My heart sank. Meg had always been a sensible person, but she was in a vulnerable time in her life. Who had gotten to her, I wondered. She saw my frown. "Don't worry!" she said. "It's a good thing. Here's what happened. I was driving in my car and listening to a radio preacher—but it wasn't the usual kind. The preacher *didn't* say that if I would just believe Jesus was the one and only Son of God, my personal savior, who died for my sins, I would be saved. He said everybody is a child of God—everyone can be like Christ. I was so excited I talked back to the radio, 'That's what I believe! I believe everyone can be a savior and that we can save the world by loving it and each other.'

"He validated the thoughts I had come to privately. It mattered to hear him say it publicly. Then it came over me in a rush that if I believed everyone was a child of God, it meant that *I was a child of God.* If anyone could be a savior of the world, then *I could be a savior of the world.* I felt a great sense of love surrounding me, surrounding everything, and I felt like the whole purpose of my life had suddenly become clear.

"When I woke up the next morning, I still felt great love all around me. I decided to try to bring this love into every encounter during the day. To help myself, I started each morning by sitting quietly to meditate and concentrate my awareness on love. I created an altar to help me remember my sense of purpose. I put up a picture of earth from outer space. I arranged a vase of fresh flowers. I lit candles. I'd become peaceful and focused. But the minute I'd get into my daily routine, it would all fall apart. I'd go to the grocery store, the checkout person would annoy me, and I would forget that she was a child of God and that I was a savior of the world. How was I going to stay focused on love and put it into practice?

"I realized I just couldn't do this alone. I needed to find some *other* people who were trying to put love into practice. Then it hit me, *church!* That is what church is for!"

Apart from Sunday school in her childhood, Megan was un-churched. She set out to find a religious community. It proved to be challenging. First, Megan went back to the liberal congregation where she'd been taken as a child. "This church *sounded* right," she observed. "The sermon was stimulating intellectually, and it addressed something that mattered: racial justice." But the congregation was all white, the music was staid, and the atmosphere was cold; the church didn't appear to be embodying what it was preaching. Disappointed, Megan decided to try a progressive, multiracial, historically black Baptist church. "This church *felt* right," Meg said, "The gospel music rocked, people were warm and welcoming, but the *words* were wrong. The sermon repeated the theology I found appalling: Jesus died to save me from my sins."

Next, Megan went to a New Age church with a multiracial congregation and small covenant groups. The groups met every week to support each other in living out their values and took on a service project together. "This church *did* right. The small groups were great, but the theology..." Meg hesitated before pronouncing her verdict, "was pabulum. We memorized affirmations about the power of mind over matter. You can't just *think* poverty, and war, and the environmental crisis away. That's nonsense."

Megan knew what kind of congregation she needed: one with the intellectual depth and social ethics of the liberal church; the warm connection with other people, the diversity, and the gospel music of the Baptist church; and the small groups and practical service of the New Age church. For Megan, it all came together when she found a progressive Jewish synagogue. The congregation emphasizes the value of silence, meditation, and spiritual practice. The Shabbat services include beautiful chanting; Torah study is engaged and intellectually rich; and the warmth of community adds joy. After a rigorous process of study and preparation, Megan converted to Judaism and joined this congregation. The simple blessings of abundant life, anchored through religious community with its networks of support and its rituals that honor the passages of life, are shared by Megan and her community. She is not adrift, not bereft, and her life's purpose is supported and amplified by a community devoted to choosing life, practicing compassion, and loving this world enough to save it.

And save it we must. It is clear that tremendous change must happen for U.S. society to end its attachment to a level of consumption that is putting the environment at risk. In the decades ahead, religious communities will be critical contexts for personal and collective transformation. Good religious communities convert people to the way of life our society needs to move to: from believing that violence is redemptive to practicing justice and compassion; from going it alone to giving and receiving care from others; from isolating oneself in individualism to sharing work on behalf of the common good.

Much in our dominant culture can lull people into numbness, complacency, or compliance. Staying awake, becoming active rather than passive in the world, requires something more of us—something we cannot do alone. Religious communities can enable people to claim and deepen the values that the dominant culture is ignoring or denying. They can convert us from lifestyles that disregard the earth and are heedless of the environmental damage and danger we are courting, to lifestyles of reverence and gratitude that enable us to be less materialistic and more attentive to the goodness of life's intangibles. They can free us from consuming unsatisfying intellectual junk food and give us deep nourishment through the bread and wine of spiritual traditions, sacred texts, intellectual quests, meditation, and prayer. Thich Nhat Hanh writes:

> I hope to see communities like that everywhere, as a kind of demonstration that life is possible, a future is possible. …There are many things that regulate us, rob us of our serenity, our peace, our time, ourselves. So, a community that shows abundance of life, that is an example of the wholeness of life, would be an eloquent sign of the possibility of the future.

This is how churches, synagogues, sanghas, and mosques make a home for hope. Their sheltering walls offer us a way of living that finds joy and meaning in each other, in simpler ways of being, in slowing down, and in giving time to the things that matter most. They enable us to create a good life together—a community of resistance, a covenant of joyful interdependence—that will support us through the radical changes needed in U.S. society as we embrace the calling to live peacefully and sustainably on this earth.

CHAPTER FOUR

Restoring Heartwood

John Buehrens

In the mid-1970s, with the bicentennial of the American Revolution approaching, sociologist Robert Bellah wrote a book called *The Broken Covenant*. It suggested that "in the beginning, and to some extent ever since, Americans have interpreted their history as having religious meaning. They saw themselves as being a 'people' in the classical and biblical sense of the word. They hoped they were a people of God."

He was implying that in failing to "live out the promise of its creed, that all men are created equal," as Dr. King had put it, and in becoming polarized over the war in Vietnam and over race and gender issues and much more, Americans had broken covenant not only with one another but with the dream, the hope, that they most had in common. The point seems even more relevant today.

The American War of Independence came from a sense of broken covenant between the colonies and their imperial masters back in Great Britain. Ministers in Massachusetts preached repeatedly on the theme. In the spring of 1775, some served as chaplains to their local militia and Minutemen. Others allowed the town munitions to be stored in the parsonage or meeting-house. And when the British army sent troops to confiscate such supplies in Lexington and Concord, the local militias all responded. Needham was a small town, but it lost five mili-tiamen on April 19, 1775. The next day, the Reverend Samuel West of First Parish had the unenviable task of calling on five widows and their total of thirty-five children. "I visited with these families immediately," he wrote in his journal, "and with a sympathetic sense of their affliction I gave some the first intel-ligence they had of the dreadful event, the death of a Husband and a Parent. The very different manner in which the tidings were received, discovered the very different disposition of the sufferers. While some were almost frantic in their grief, others received the news with profound silence."

The recent renovation of our historic meetinghouse ex-posed to view for a time some of its massive oaken framework beams. They date back to the 1773 structure in which West did his preaching. Strong, gnarled, twisted, in places broken and repaired, they held the meetinghouse together even when it was put up on log rollers and moved across town. These framework beams, each about a foot square and thirty feet long, are hewn from the heart of oaks that were already big and old when they were cut down. There is something awesome in their grain and tensions. Writer Scott Russell Sanders once put it eloquently in an essay he called "Heartwood."

> Trees breathe, my father taught me. They draw in what we cast off, carbon dioxide, and they give off what we crave, oxygen, and so our breath circles in and out of their pores. Only the outer bark of a tree is alive, the tender inch or two of sapwood just beneath the bark which carries vital juices between dirt and leaves. The inner core of the tree,

the heartwood, is no longer living. It's not really dead, but merely still, finished, like a snapshot. Sliced open, the heartwood reveals a tree's history. So the grain exposed on our walls and floors and furnishings tells of the fat years and thin, weather hard and mild, soils deep and shallow. The texture of each board is like the photograph of a face bearing marks from a lifetime of blessings and blows.

Each plank in our floor is unique, and yet when the planks are laid side by side they resemble one another like brothers and sisters, faithful to the design of oaks. If the universe itself has a design, some deep and steadfast grain that reveals the kinship among all its parts, then what could be more important for a life's work than trying to discern that pattern? All of science is based on the faith that there is such a grain in things, at least in everything that can be measured. But what of those immeasurable things—feeling and thought, memory and longing, actions and words—is there a grain to them as well? Is there a pattern in our striving, a moral to be drawn from this history of breath?

Perhaps there is. Like Martin Buber, I believe that we humans are not so much homo sapiens (we are neither that wise nor that self-aware), but rather we are the "promise-making, promise-breaking, promise-renewing animal." We ourselves are created in the context of relationships, promises, commitments. We then either break them, make new ones, modify them, or renew them. To use a word deeply rooted in our culture, we are "covenantal" by nature. It's in our grain, our heartwood. And all authentic covenants are created, sustained, and renewed in authentic hope.

We like to think of ourselves as self-created. But we are not. No more than are the oaks from the forests primeval of New England that became the beams of the meetinghouse. If we forget this, as human beings so easily do, then we easily become like the scoundrel politician my mother was once forced by social circumstance to shake hands with. When asked why she found him so distasteful, she replied, "Why, he's nothing but another self-made man who worships his own creator!"

This was the late senator Joseph McCarthy, who had slandered others repeatedly in public to appear to be saving and protecting us all. That pattern repeats itself, of course. Finally McCarthy was censured for breaking covenant with his oath of office and with Senate ethics. Was he ever repentant? I can't pretend to know.

All I can be sure of is that one of the functions of authentic religion is to allow us to restore our own heartwood and renew the covenants and the promise that we have failed to fulfill. In the first congregation I served, for example, we often began worship and affirmed our reason for gathering by saying together, "Mindful of truth ever exceeding our knowledge, of love and compassion ever exceeding our practice, reverently we covenant together, beginning with ourselves as we are, to share the strength of integrity and the heritage of the spirit, in humanity's unending quest for reality, justice, and love."

I like those phrases still. But I also realize that the very concept of covenant can easily become misused, broken, or twisted. Take its use in real estate law: when property is conveyed with a so-called "restrictive covenant," the attempt is to exclude certain groups of buyers or uses deemed undesirable. But there is a deep difference between a legal contract (of any sort) and an authentic spiritual covenant, as I often explain to the couples who ask me to preside at their weddings.

"There is a legal dimension to marriage," I say. "And important civil protections. You will go to the courthouse and get a license. I will sign it, just before the ceremony. Then I may seal it up, throw it in the corner, and holler, 'Render unto Caesar the things that are Caesar's!'—because there is a deeper spiritual meaning to your relationship. Then we will all step out, and, before God and everyone, celebrate your spiritual covenant with one another. It's not primarily a contract at all. Contracts arise from distrust, worries, and what-ifs, and are often full of penalty clauses. But the core of the spiritual covenant between you lies in the trust and love that you have found in one another, in your gratitude, and in the commitment that you make to care, not only for one another, but also for your relationship, to seek to renew it when challenged."

Hope is key to every covenant. As I have told my congregation, which takes pride in a heritage of being non-creedal, our forebears were wise in putting aside creedal questions, "What do we all believe in common? What ancient formulae of faith are we willing to confess together?" in favor of the more covenantal questions: "What spiritual hopes do we share? What shall we promise to one another and to God as we try to live together toward our hopes? How shall we then try to treat one another?" But I sometimes worry that in taking pride in their non-creedal freedom they can easily forget the deep responsibilities that their freedom—if it is truly covenantal freedom— necessarily entails.

Martin Buber once told a parable to illustrate this point. In the beginning of the modern world, he said, around the time of the American and French Revolutions, three ideals were said to walk hand in hand: *liberty, equality,* and what was then named *fraternity,* which we might today better called human *kinship.* Then something happened. In the turmoil of revolutions and time, the three became separated. Liberty went west—to America first of all. But alone it changed its character, said Buber, becoming mere freedom without responsibility—freedom to exploit the land, to exploit other human beings, and freedom from community and from obligation rather than the freedom to fulfill an inherent purpose or promise. Equality went east, and it also changed. It became the equality of the *gulag*, the equality of the masses all waving the same "Little Red Book." Meanwhile, the sense of authentic human kinship went into hiding. As the most religious of the three ideals, kinship became disparaged by the secular elites. So it hid in the religious lives of people suffering oppression. But when there were efforts to restore some equality of opportunity to America's vaunted freedoms, as in the civil rights movement, it reemerged. When there were efforts to restore some authentic covenantal freedom—of worship, of conscience, of speech, of association—to socialist equality, as in the Solidarity movement of Poland, there it was again, reuniting the separated.

I have become convinced that something analogous is happening in current efforts to restore the heartwood of Western culture and its deep sense of covenant. Among the three spiritual virtues, *faith, hope, and love,* again a mediating term, *hope,* seems key to the restoration. The other two have too often been seized and distorted by extremists. Faith need not be fundamentalism, but faith per se is as distrusted by many on the Left as liberal appeals to love are dismissed on the Right as mere sentimental blather. No wonder so many attempts to restore and strengthen civil society, from Vaclav Havel's Prague to Barack Obama's campaign for the U.S. presidency, have appealed first to hope. But what we need most to understand is that authentic hope cannot be simply an appetite; it needs to be a restoration of deep and covenantal humility.

Hope that is based on personal, political, or group pride is often headed for a fall. As Andrew Delbanco writes in *The Real American Dream: A Meditation on Hope,* the Puritans were wise in teaching that "pride is the enemy of hope." He says that he relearned that lesson while researching the spirituality behind Alcoholics Anonymous. That organization, too, has a covenant grounded more in shared human experience and hope than in any particular creedal theology. Yet it wisely passes on a form of spiritual wisdom that resembles that of the Puritan divine who said that "a holy despaire in ourselves is the ground of true hope."

Too much liberal and modernist religion, I fear, is all too likely not only to forget that ground, but even to think that covenantal relations are simply a matter of our own intentionality, and not a gift—what the Puritans called "a covenant of grace," rather than one of works. In the biblical tradition, after all, the most basic covenants were initiatives not on the part of human beings, but on the part of God, starting with the covenant of being itself, the Creation. It was then renewed in covenant with the legendary Noah when God, having despaired of us, renews hope in humankind and promises not to try to destroy the world again but to hope that we can somehow learn to care for the earth and for one another. Abraham, the first to forgo idolatry, enters into a covenant full of hope and promise; one that is renewed when some of his descendants are freed from their slavery in Egypt.

Jewish tradition says that God tried to persuade other, more powerful nations to enter into a spiritual covenant of freedom and responsibility. But none would willingly enter into any obligations. So the covenant offered at Sinai went to the poor, oppressed Hebrews, who, having escaped from bondage, essentially promised not to treat one another the way that they had been treated, and not to treat anyone else that way either. Not that they always lived up to the commandments; although God is faithful, human beings are far less so. Here in America, for example, the colonies formed a nation with a constitution as a contract or compact between the states, under which slavery was at first not only perpetuated, but even protected. It took a civil war, with Lincoln at Gettysburg reinvoking the covenantal hope of the Declaration of Independence, to bring about what he called "a new birth of freedom." He was not merely nostalgic for its ideals. Rather he renewed and restored them in what has been called a form of "innovative nostalgia."

So what shall we do with the twisted, broken, fractured framework of covenant that is our spiritual inheritance in America? Shall we simply chop it all up and burn it, because it has been broken? Because *we* have broken it? I write this on a winter night in New England, sitting by my fireplace, warmed for the moment by the heat from the fire, remembering a mentor who often cited the ancient Hindu proverb, "Do not cut down and destroy the Wisdom Tree."

It is one thing to tell people in a time when the dominant religious establishment has been corrupted, "Bear good fruit worthy of repentance," as John the Baptist did. "Even now the ax is lying at the root of the trees; every tree there that does not bear good fruit is cut down and thrown into the fire."

But modernity has been guilty all too often of hacking away indiscriminately at the Wisdom Tree, tearing it up root and branch, leaving a wilderness. So much so that one characteristic of the postmodern turn our culture is now taking is that it finally admits that it needs the framework, grain, support, and direction of spiritual wisdom—though it is just as likely to turn East, beyond the covenantal tradition, for guidance. They forget that one who studies covenantal wisdom is like "a tree planted by the waters" and that in the Christian scriptures this tree appears again in the vision of a heavenly city, where "the leaves of the tree are for the healing of the nations."

Covenant as a concept is not just about commitment to a particular community. Because of its connection to hope, it is also about a community's commitment to a vision without which we all perish. For after all, from a God's eye point of view, earth remains one world, very much as a favorite hymn puts it, "one as covenants can build it."

True covenantal hope always has such a perspective—it is always a bit utopian, yearning for the realization of God's kingdom here on earth, for millennial fulfillment. The Puritan mission to this end was too often narcissistic, forgetting those who were here before them and taking the wilderness for granted as something they alone could turn into paradise. They should have been far more self-critical. That is a key role of religion: to hold up critical standards. After the American Revolution, this broken covenantal heritage of hope was then blended with a more utilitarian and populist republicanism. Robert Bellah was right when he suggested that the radicalism of authentic covenantal hope is necessary to subvert our too easy, liberal complacency with any status quo—if we are ever to fulfill the promise of our heritage: the promise of covenantal, democratic community in right relation with others and with the creation. And that hope must now be both global in its vision and local in its realization. Let me offer a few illustrations that come to mind.

When my congregation in Needham decided to renovate the old meetinghouse   with new and expanded spaces for our own congregational uses as well as a day-care center and meeting rooms for Alcoholics Anonymous, civic organizations, and public education, with handicapped accessibility and with green design a top priority—we learned that we would have to vacate the premises for an entire year. What! Where would we go? Where would we hold worship services, pursue religious education, have offices, convene youth group and other meetings, do counseling, and so on? We tried public schools. Many communities allow religious groups to temporarily rent space in the schools. The main rule is equal access. Not in our town! Despite the fact that a Needham school building was once leased for five years to a Jewish religious school, we were denied even the opportunity to share office space with the local historical society—because it leases the land under its building from the town. "Church-state separation," we were then told. Short of suing, I could only sigh over a misapplication of a principle I generally support.

At my most despairing, I approached the rabbi of our local Reform synagogue. Would his congregation possibly let us worship and have a few classes in the synagogue building? That community is booming, with four hundred children in religious school Sunday mornings. Rabbi Perlman's response was covenantal: he asked his lay leaders to study with him the passages in Genesis 18 in which Abraham is approached by three strangers looking for hospitality. Together they paid attention to the anomalies in the text, as good rabbis do, and read that Abraham first "sat," then "saw," then "ran" to meet them; then "hastened" to have hospitality prepared; and then "stood" by the guests while they were fed and refreshed. Finally, they noticed that while they had seemed to greet only human strangers, the encounter becomes one with the Other, with G-d. As I sat by, the rabbi then finished the *Dvar Torah*, the scriptural study, by telling the leaders of Temple Beth Shalom, "So, since what we've seen is that the question is not *whether* we should welcome our friends and neighbors from First Parish, but rather *how quickly* we can hasten to welcome them, let's now shift our attention to what would make that possible for all concerned."

Interfaith cooperation, as we will see further on, is often a matter of covenant. We then were guests at the synagogue's Passover seder, at which the leaders of both congregations signed a *berith*, a formal covenant, promising not only to share sacred space but to learn from one another and to grow in service to the wider community. We hung a copy of that covenant in the entry of the temple for everyone to see. And every time I look at it I am reminded that, just as the covenantal framework of my congregation and its meetinghouse is its oldest, strongest, and most enduring element, so there is reason to believe that covenantal renewal is what is most needed today not only in progressive religion in America but in the progressive movement generally.

Even such secular political thinkers as Marcus Raskin clearly see this. In his book *Liberalism: The Genius of American Ideals*, this staunch progressive speaks of the need for a liberalism of "reconstruction." Like thinkers as different as Cornel West, Bellah, and Delbanco, he charts a clear line of descent from the Puritan covenant of grace, formed in hope, through the radical reformers of the nineteenth century—the abolitionists, utopians, and suffragists—through the pragmatism of William James and John Dewey and the progressive movements of the twentieth century, and up to the present. Raskin includes a chapter titled "The Liberal Democratic Covenant: Everyone Sits at the Table," and he ends with an appendix reprinting both the Universal Declaration of Human Rights and the International Covenant on Economic, Social, and Cultural Rights.

Progressive religion in America is needed to remind America of its highest hopes and ideals and of what its heartwood concept of covenant most basically teaches: that authentic hope can never be merely individualistic or self-developed. It has a social and transcendent dimension. But it does need to be renewed and strengthened within human hearts and communities through a form of what has been called "the dialectic of covenant and conversion," first practiced by the earliest churches of America.

One of the great theologians of progressive religion in the twentieth century, social ethicist James Luther Adams, often warned liberals that the weakness of commitment that they would complain about in others was a direct result of their own undervaluing the importance of conversion—of what the Hebrew Bible calls *teshuvah* and the Christian scriptures call *metanoia.*

In her spiritual autobiography, *Traveling Mercies,* Anne Lamott, herself a convert to progressive religion, talks about why she insists that her son Sam go with her to church. She knows that this is hardly common practice among her left-leaning friends, and it is not always popular with Sam himself—at least not until he gets there.

"The main reason [I make him go]," she writes, "is that I want to give him what I found in the world, which is to say, a path and a little light to see by. Most of the people I know who have what I want, which is to say, purpose, heart, balance, gratitude, joy, are people with a deep sense of spirituality. They are people in community, who pray or practice their faith, they are Buddhists, Jews, Christians, people banding together to work on themselves and for human rights. They follow a brighter light than the glimmer of their own candle, they are part of something beautiful."

This is what we do in progressive religion. In the midst of an economic system that increasingly treats human beings as expendable "deadwood," we insist on restoring heartwood. We offer a framework of covenantal commitment. We live by shared hope. We make a path by walking it—not alone, together. And we pray that along the way, those who walk with us will be converted and will make a deep personal commitment to its radical form of hope—not for themselves alone, but for everyone.

PART THREE

The Roof

CHAPTER FIVE

Deliver Us from Evil

Rebecca Parker

In the heat of the day or the cold of the storm, people need a roof over their heads. "Been in the storm too long," an old song laments, testifying to the tattered hearts and worn-down spirits of human beings left unprotected from harsh conditions. The travails that ravage life are many: war, poverty, cruelty, deprivation, prejudice, abuse. In the hells made by humans, is there something that can salve the wounds or stop the injury? What can protect life from harm? How can hearts and bodies and communities broken by injustice be restored? How do we come to terms with the presence of what can be called evil? And who, or what, will answer the prayer, "Deliver us from evil"?

The roof of our theological house is a metaphor for salvation—for safe haven from that which threatens life. In the church I go to most Sundays, carved redwood rafters hold up the roof. When I'm most weary or worried, I gaze up at the rafters and find comfort in their strength—as if God had taken material form and was arching over the people seeking sanctuary from the storm. All people need a framework of meaning by which to negotiate the "many dangers, toils, and snares" that confront their lives. Our frameworks support us when threats come. They even shape *what* threats we see and guide what response we choose as trustworthy or wise.

In Christian theology, the familiar teaching about evil and salvation takes the form of a story. Evil entered the world at the start, when Satan tempted Eve in the garden to disobey God's commandments. Eve persuaded Adam to join her in eating the forbidden fruit, and because of the sinful disobedience of humanity's first parents, all subsequent generations have been born tainted by sin. God punished humanity for Adam and Eve's transgression by exiling humanity from the garden of paradise and closing its gates. Disasters followed. Brothers killed brothers; nations went to war against nations; folly, sin, and evil multiplied. God finally intervened by sending Jesus—his own son—into the world to die on the cross to atone for humanity's sins. Those who accept him as their savior receive the benefits of his saving death. His torment on the cross frees them from having to be eternally punished. After death, they will go to heaven—the final reward for those who have been saved.

In this salvation story, the source of evil is outside of human beings, in the evil serpent—an image for Satan, the devil, or tempter—who counters God's commands and tempts human beings to join him. Evil is a force that opposes God, is active in this world, and leads human beings to sin. Sin is disobedience of God's commands, and all humanity is guilty. We inherit guilt from the generations before us. Our sinful nature means we deserve eternal punishment. Salvation, too, comes from outside of human beings, through the atoning death of Jesus on the cross.

This salvation story, believed by many, is not the only salvation story told in Christianity. But it has dominated much of the past thousand years of Western Christian history. It is sung in gospel hymns, retold in sermons, and displayed in images. Progressive religion has critiqued the limits and problems of this theology and offers alternatives. The critique focuses on two points: (1) the doctrine of Jesus's atoning death has functioned to sanction violence and to bless suffering as good—with tragic results; and (2) attributing evil to Satan and defining sin as disobedience to God lets human beings off the hook for our responsibility for causing harm to one another and the earth. The alternative theology of salvation emphasizes (1) that human beings need to be saved from the consequences of human sin—not from God's punishing wrath; and (2) that salvation comes through the powers of life and goodness, present within and around us. Jesus saves by the beauty of his life and teachings, by incarnating God's presence. He died because of evil and sin. His resurrection—which does not have to be understood literally—reveals that the powers of life and love can counter and even, sometimes, defeat the effects of evil. In sum, the liberal theological perspective emphasizes that both sin and salvation, evil and the redemption of evil, are in our hands. Though they take transpersonal forms in social structures and systems, as well as personal forms in the choices we make for ourselves, both sin and salvation involve the exercise of human powers. We do not carry our powers in isolation, however. Resources of healing, resistance, and survival permeate life—gifts of God's grace. By these we are sustained and from these we can draw to use our powers to counter evil with good.

Recognizing and naming the limits of the traditional doctrine of the atonement is a defining feature of progressive Christianity. The classic doctrine of the atonement says violence will protect us. The violent death of Jesus, in fulfillment of God's will, becomes an image of how life can be protected by sacrifice, by redemptive suffering, in response to a God who uses violence to punish and destroy evil. But when God is viewed as saving the world through a violent act, theology functions to justify human violence. Victims of violence believe their suffering is God's will, and perpetrators of violence can believe they are imitating God's way of salvation when they "punish" evildoers.

Consider, for example, that in the spring of 2004, while the United States bombed Iraq and the war's casualty toll climbed, images of the lacerated body of Christ filled the film screens of America. Mel Gibson's *Passion of the Christ* reproduced medieval Christianity's images of Jesus's torture and execution in Technicolor, presenting violence both as divinely sanctioned, necessary for salvation, and as an occasion for gratitude and awe. Gibson's film arrived just in time to bathe the conscience of a nation at war in the assertion that Christ's sacrificial death revealed God's love. Cadets at the U.S. Air Force Academy in Colorado Springs who were shown the film were exposed to a theology not unlike what the twelfth-century crusaders heard from Peter the Hermit when he "preached the cross" in the towns and cities of Europe, inviting recruits to serve Christ by offering themselves to kill or be killed in Jesus's name. They were enjoined to be part of Team Jesus, encouraged by evangelical Christian organizations based in Colorado Springs, such as Focus on the Family and the Officers' Christian Fellowship, that were closely involved with the Air Force Academy. In the movie, as in medieval art, Mary displayed the ideal response for mothers, according to her assigned role within the patriarchal family: she suffers silently with her son but raises no outcry to stop or protest the Father's divine will.

It is disturbing how often those who believe in Jesus's redemptive sacrifice on the cross imitate that violence by sacrificing lives to purify their world. Serving God through violence has a thousand-year history in Western Christianity. Rita Na-kashima Brock and I discuss that history in detail in *Saving Paradise*. We trace it back to changes in the observance of the ritual of the Eucharist: in the ninth century, it started to shift from a feast of life to a reenactment of the killing of Jesus. These changes, originating in the court of Charlemagne, were followed by the emergence of Crucifixion imagery in Christian art in the tenth century and by Christianity's turn in the eleventh century to holy war and to a formal theology of Christ's atoning death. The pious practices and spirituality of those who embraced Crucifixion-centered theology offered an ideological framework that assisted imperial strategies to unify Europe through the identification and violent subjugation of ethnic Others.

The doctrine of the atonement also has tragic results in life's more intimate spheres. Early in my experience as a minister, a woman whose husband was beating her came to me for counsel. She said she'd consulted her priest many years before and he'd told her to rejoice in her sufferings because they brought her closer to Jesus. Just as Jesus bore the humiliation and pain of the cross out of love for humanity, if she truly loved her husband, she'd accept his blows. For many years, she followed her priest's advice, but when her husband began to hit her children she wanted a second opinion. I struggled with myself for a moment before answering her. I had just preached a sermon on love, saying love "bears all things" and will never give up on loving another no matter what the personal cost. Her question made me realize a different framework was needed, for her and for me. When I found my voice to answer her I said, "What your priest told you is not true. God wants you to protect your life and your children's lives, not sacrifice them." She smiled and said, "Good! I knew I was right!" Beginning that day, she took steps that freed her and her children from an abusive situation. It took a new theological framework for her to survive.

Another example: a friend who was sexually abused by her father for much of her childhood told me that as a child she lived to go to church on Sunday. There she heard sermons about Jesus, the tortured victim of sin, whose death saved the world. She identified with Jesus and took comfort when his suffering was praised in word and song. She felt that she, like Jesus, was condemned by her father to humiliation and pain, but if Jesus' suffering redeemed the world, her suffering might also save someone or something. This framework of meaning gave her solace and helped her endure, but it also kept her captive. Her religion gave her no theological support for believing that her father's abuse was wrong or that she had a right to protection from it. To heal and thrive, she had to construct a different framework of meaning.

Liberal religion recognizes that a different theology of sin and salvation is needed if religion is to offer genuine solace and healing, and if it is to empower human beings in the struggle against violence, abuse, oppression, and war. The alternative begins by reimagining how sin and evil are understood. Sin has classically been defined as rebellion against God's sovereign will. But rebellious human beings who resist submission to unjust systems are often defenders of life and liberty. Their rebellion is hardly the root of all evil. Progressive women, rereading the Genesis story through the eyes of their own experience, have identified with Eve's curiosity, boldness, and willingness to risk punishment rather than abandon their reach for what the serpent said the tree could provide: knowledge. When religion labels Eve—who didn't follow the rules laid down by a male God—to be the face of evil, it puts women and girls at risk and gives men license to imitate God in acts that exclude, condemn, or punish women. But Eve can be seen another way. She wasn't the first sinner, biblical scholar Phyllis Trible has suggested, but the first theologian. Eve is the original brave questioner, willing to transgress the established order to grasp the apple of learning. Progressive religion celebrates Eve as an exemplar of women claiming their full humanity, which includes their intellectual life and their right to an education. Eve would bless and support the young girls in Afghanistan I read about recently in the news. Acid was thrown in their faces when they were on their way to school. One of them said, "The people who did this to me don't want women to be educated. They want us to be stupid things." But the girls returned to school. They stood up to evil, refusing to be kept in a place of submission and ignorance.

The liberal theologian Walter Rauschenbusch rejected the notion that humanity's rebellion against God's rule is the root cause of all sin. "When theological definitions speak of rebellion against God as the common characteristic of all sin," he wrote, "it reminds one of the readiness of despotic governments to treat every offence as treason." He asserted in contrast that "our universe is not a despotic monarchy with God above the starry canopy and ourselves down here; it is a spiritual commonwealth with God in the midst of us." For him, sin is not the betrayal of God's rules but the betrayal of one another. Sin matters not because it disappoints, offends, or alienates God, but because it destroys life-giving relationships of love and justice in human affairs—leaving tragedy and broken hearts in its wake. For Rauschenbusch, self-centeredness is the root cause of our failures of each other. When selfishness is regarded as the root of all evil, as it is for Social Gospel Christians of Rauschenbusch's lineage, unselfish love for others opens the path of salvation. Self-sacrifice, love's most perfect form, saves.

Progressive women and theologians of color have gone further. They have noted that social systems often unequally distribute the imperative of sacrifice. In patriarchal society, male privileges and power are sustained by women who sacrifice for men and for their children. In white-supremacy culture, white privilege and power are sustained through the sacrifice of people of color. In military-industrial societies, the economic elite are helped economically by war, and the majority of those who die in battle are poor or lower-middle-class people "giving their lives for their country"; of them, a disproportionate number are people of color. Self-sacrifice is not sufficient to transform evil. Sometimes, self-sacrifice sustains social structures that benefit some at the expense of others. There is no virtue in this.

What is evil? Evil is that which exploits the lives of some to benefit the lives of others. Evil congregates in transpersonal systems, in social structures that run on banal visions of the good life, lacking in wisdom or zest, and beneficial to some while leaving others bereft of life's necessities. Evil springs from ignorance and denial of the beauty and goodness of life. It chooses ways of living that destroy rather than sustain the delicate web of relationships that make life possible. Evil's accomplice is anesthetization. When the senses have been numbed, and feeling has been stifled, responsive reverence is dulled, and love has no air to breathe. Evil is manifest in sexism, racism, and militarism and in patterns of exploitation and abuse. Its harm touches our innermost being and our relationships with one another and the earth. Evil corrodes our inner lives, manifesting in self-hatred, powerlessness, and fragmentation of the soul. Its effects are present in hunger, homelessness, and refugee camps, in the suffering of soldiers experiencing post-traumatic stress, or the wrenching grief of families who have lost loved ones to war. The consequences of evil are displayed by trouble in earth's ecosystems—disappearing species, melting ice caps, the thinning ozone.

Liberal and progressive theologies emphasize that these are

the great threats to our lives and to future generations. Life needs to be saved from the harm that sin and evil cause in this world. The tragic consequences of sin are of our making. God is not our biggest threat, and we don't need to be saved from the danger that God will eternally punish us for our sins. Rather, earth itself needs salvation from damage made by us humans; humanity needs healing and repair from legacies of injustice. We are the cause, and we can be the cure.

Evil can be neither denied nor destroyed. It is a perennial in the garden. It has to be astutely recognized and unmasked. The early Christians provided training in resistance to evil, and they understood that evil operated in three primary modes: fraud, pomp, and greed. Ritual played a key role in symbolizing the struggle with evil and in providing the religious community with resources for the ongoing and arduous work of resisting evil. Exorcism required physical, emotional, and psychological effort—on a communal level.

People of liberal faith might do well to update this ancient understanding of evil. Devouring and destructive power rarely is seen in overt maliciousness or unmasked cruelty. It operates within and behind masks—and its fraud fools even those who wear its mask. Resisting evil requires advanced wisdom, courage, and skill at unmasking deception, evading being duped or tempted, standing grounded in things of greater value than prestige in the eyes of others, and recognizing abundance, rather than running on an imagined emptiness and seeking to accumulate more than is needed.

Evil is not mysterious, not insignificant, and not rare. It is ordinary, life-destroying, and pervasive. It cannot be confined to evildoers and enemies whose destruction will please God and free us. Calmness in the face of evil comes to those who, rather than being frantic to purge it, concentrate their attention on recognizing and resisting its habits. This is the gift of age, of elders, of long-practiced care for life. Innocence of evil, purity from evil—these are illusions or temporary states of the very young. Innocence and purity are not states of salvation. Salvation manifests in wisdom, persistence, in not allowing evil to operate in its habitual patterns. It manifests as a solid sense of "enough," in gratitude for life's goodness, showing a humble capacity to be part of the web of life. The blessings of salvation are evident in those who hold tragedy and beauty together, integrating life's complex and difficult counterpoints within a strong heart that bears reality with love and moral clarity.

How is evil countered and its harm redressed or stopped? There are alternatives to theologies of redemption through violence. In Christian tradition, the alternatives can be found in early Christianity itself and in countermovements to the dominant trend toward Crucifixion-centered theologies of Christianity's second millennium. Salvation comes through the gift of human powers and capacities, used to heal injury, comfort the afflicted, create justice, and offer love. Early Christian theologians taught that humanity's powers and capacities were restored to their potential for good by the incarnation of God in human form. Through Christ's incarnation, God resanctified humanity, rekindling the divine spark in souls. In his life and teachings, Jesus exemplified how humanity's gifts can be used to bless rather than curse, to heal rather than hurt, to counter the injustices of a dominating empire through loving one's neighbor as oneself.

In this understanding of salvation, those who join themselves to the living Christ, through the ritual of baptism, take on the calling to be saviors and do the work of salvation. They are to be Christs in this world, as Cyril of Jerusalem put it in his fourth-century instructions to Christian converts. Christians are anointed like Jesus, imbued with the spirit of life, to

heal the sick, release the captive, feed the hungry, and taste and
see the goodness of God in this world.

Being attuned to beauty, with ones senses alive and alert,
helps save us. In early Christian worship practices, those who
took part in the Eucharist ritual would touch their eyes and
ears and nostrils with fingers dipped in the communion wine.
"Everything belongs to the God of beauty," an early Christian prayer states. Centuries later, Rūmī would write, "Let the
beauty we love become the good we do."

Life is protected and saved by those who embody presence,
wisdom, resistance, gratitude, and humility. These are the gifts
people can bring to one another and can foster through long
participation and practice as members of religious communities devoted to saving and protecting life, rooted in rituals of
praise and thanksgiving. Through such communities, humanity's divine capacities can be honed in the service of life and be
trained to unmask and resist evil.

On a dusty roadside outside Crawford, Texas, in the summer of
2005, Celeste Zappala stood with many others who had come to
ask the vacationing president of the United States what justified the deaths of their family members in the Iraq War. Celeste
was there because she'd made a promise at her son's graveside
that she would not be silent about the lies that had sent him
to war and caused his death. The U.S. government's reasons for
going to war had been revealed as "deceitful masks"—the term
Augustine used in *City of God* in protesting a war in another
time:

> This war was kindled only in order that there "might sound
> in languid ears the cry of victory." Away then with these de-
> ceitful masks, these deluding whitewashes, that things may
> be truthfully seen and scrutinized.

Celeste Zappala's son, Sherwood Baker, was a young father when his National Guard unit was sent to Iraq. He'd joined the guard to contribute to his community and to help pay for his student loans. As a child growing up, he was "big and loud and wonderful," his mother said. On April 26, 2004—just seven weeks after he was deployed—he was one of two soldiers killed in an explosion in Baghdad. Celeste Zappala recounts how she received the news:

> I was preparing dinner in the kitchen. The front door was open. It was raining and I didn't have the porch light on. Our dog started barking and lunging for the door. I went to the porch and saw a man standing there with a notebook. At first I thought he must be selling magazines. Then I began to see the medals. He said, are you Sherwood's mother? Are you Sherwood's mother? And I just started to scream and scream and scream.

Celeste Zappala transgressed the role culturally assigned to mothers when she and Cindy Sheehan founded Gold Star Mothers for Peace and began publicly protesting the deaths of their sons in Iraq. Their noncompliant grief called into question the unfettered performance of war. Such an outcry against violence harks back to premedieval Christian art. In the fifth-century basilica of Santa Maria Maggiore in Rome, the arch mosaic includes a depiction of the slaughter of the innocents, the story told in Luke of Herod's massacre of all boys under two years of age in his effort to kill the Christ child. The mosaic shows mothers with wild, unbound hair—a sign of grief—gathered before Herod's throne. They hold their sons in their arms, a crowd of women mourners facing a violent tyrant. These mothers, like the twentieth-century mothers of the disappeared in Latin America, the contemporary women in black, and the Gold Star mothers for peace, protest imperial violence with unbounded outrage, grief channeled into protest and confrontation.

Celeste Zappala exemplifies a Christian understanding of salvation. She demonstrates a fierce love for life, and in the name of love she works to protect the goodness of life's intricate interdependence against the forces in our selves, our present society, and our cultural legacies that violate life. Love, for her, includes embracing the fullness of life, even when that fullness is experienced as grief for all that has been lost and cannot be repaired. Her actions are not those of an isolated individual, but, by her own account, are rooted in her church community, the First United Methodist Church of Germantown, Pennsylvania. In a speech thanking her congregation, she spoke of the strength she had taken from their community:

> Nothing we can write or say or do, no logic or righteousness gives us the thing we want most, the lives of our sons—the chance to see them grow old and have lots of kids, the chance to share holidays and most of all to hold them and tell them we love them. That has all passed away and believe me when I tell you that despair is a companion who always seeks us out, awaits at the corner. And the force that bows that despair is the powerful love of the community and faith that says the light does shine in the darkness and the darkness can not overcome it. We—all of us—are the powerful source of living light, along with people all over this country and this world who will stand up for peace, against despair and hatred.

Resistance to evil through acts of love and protest is more possible when people ground their lives in more than outrage and grief: in a deep affirmation of life's goodness, in celebration of life's beauty and in receptivity to grace. Albert Camus observed in The Rebel that underneath the "no" of every true protest there is a deeper "yes." The apprehension of life's goodness provides a foundation for emotional aliveness and moral clarity—it fuels outrage, protest, and social critique. At the same time, it sustains activism through refreshing experiences of beauty and joy.

Some people imagine salvation as personal escape from divine punishment in hell. Rescued by belief in Christ's sacrificial death, the saved look forward to eternal life in heaven—separated by death and by God's gracious rewards from the sin and evil of this world. Such otherworldly salvation does not overly concern itself with evil in this world except to defend against it by separating from evildoers, trying to convert them if possible and, if not, then punishing them as God would—when necessary, destroying them.

Others imagine salvation in social and this-worldly terms. It is manifested, as Martin Luther King Jr. and Social Gospel theologians such as Walter Rauschenbusch pictured it, as the realization of the dream of racial harmony and justice, the alleviation of poverty, and the end of war. The liberation of the oppressed and the overthrow of tyrants and unjust structures of power are accomplished through nonviolence, following the example of Christ, the prince of peace, whose ministry, teachings, and healings show that God's promise of salvation can be realized now.

An additional vision of salvation goes beyond hope for either heavenly reward or earthly success. It recognizes salvation as the gift of full aliveness, here and now, the restored and enlivened capacity to be in the world with wisdom. Such wisdom is not a personal accomplishment but an achievement of life together in human communities that foster astute attention to life in the present, that celebrate beauty and goodness, and that resist evil.

In this third vision, hope for salvation is something more than either idealistic commitment to building a better world, or otherworldly escape from punishment. Salvation is fully arriving in *this* life, turning our faces toward its complex realities and engaging our whole being in creative, compassionate, loving interaction with what is at hand. Salvation is the birth of full aliveness, the incarnation of divinity in the flesh of human life together. Salvation is not something one possesses individually: it is something one participates in communally, including in communion with those who have come before.

"Do you want to know how I believe we are saved?" my grandmother once asked me. "We aren't saved by Jesus's death on the cross. People who believe that focus on hocus-pocus and avoid having to live out the teachings of Jesus. We are saved by every person in every time and place that has stood up for what is true in spite of threat. Like Socrates did. Like Jesus did. Like many others have done." We are saved by the communion of saints. They shelter us, and we have the opportunity to be in their number, here and now.

CHAPTER SIX

Taking Refuge

John Buehrens

I may fully understand the Buddhist worldview only in a subsequent incarnation. Like many Americans, I am attracted to its alternative perspective on the "human problem" and its solution. According to Buddhism, as I understand it, the problem is that life is suffering (*dukkha*). The cause of suffering is desire, attachment, clinging (*samudaya*). Therefore suffering can cease (*nirodha*). And the way to overcome it is neither through self-indulgence nor extreme asceticism, but through an eightfold path (*marga*) of moderation. Those who accept this path are then said to "take refuge"—in the Buddha, the *dharma* (the teaching), and the *sangha* (the community of practice).

In this life, however, my own path is different, and I have taken refuge elsewhere. "Life is good," proclaims the cap that I wear to keep my balding head warm in the New England winter. It comes from a company of the same name founded by two brothers, Bert and John Jacobs, who grew up in my town of Needham. Even when life is also hard—and God knows that it can be—I like that affirmation. I also know where it comes from—Genesis 1:31: "God saw everything he had made, and indeed it was *very* good."

My path is one of liberal interpretation of the biblical tradition. I started my ministry as a progressive in the heart of the American Bible Belt. I took refuge in liberal understandings of the Bible out of sheer self-defense.

The critic Northrop Frye called the Bible "the great code" of Western civilization. It's the very DNA of Western culture. Even those who rejected traditional, conservative interpretations or wanted to escape it entirely were still influenced by it. One cannot possibly understand our heritage of art, music, or literature, much less our public rhetoric and politics, without understanding the Bible. When I look at the Needham meetinghouse where I preach and teach, the roofline reminds me of a huge book turned upside down over the people within. Inside, the oldest artifact—kept under the eighteenth-century plain pine communion table on the chancel—is a seventeenth-century "Bible box." Our forebears kept their most valued book in it. In case of fire, leather straps could be grabbed to save it. Those are missing now.

My job today, it seems, is to try to save the Bible from conservatives who claim to be its friends but who interpret it in oppressive ways that violate the Spirit that formed it. Conservatives are often literalists, despite the fact that scripture itself insists that "the letter kills, while the Spirit gives life." Under the roof of the old meetinghouse, I am aware that, according to traditional Christian theology, the scriptures contain "all things necessary to salvation." No wonder I associate them, and the roof above, with the part of theology known as "soteriology," from the Greek word *soteria,* meaning salvation, deliverance, preservation, or release. "Salvation" comes from the Latin word *salvus,* meaning healthy, whole.

People sometimes ask, "But what is it that we need to be

saved *from?*" I am often tempted to say, "From ourselves. From our self-involvement, and the mess we make when we forget 'right relationship' with one another, with the creation, and with the Creator." But the traditional answer is one word: sin.

That notoriously terse New Englander Calvin Coolidge supposedly went to church one Sunday morning without Mrs. Coolidge, who was at home ill with a cold. When he returned, she asked, "What was the sermon about?" "Sin," said the president. "But what did the minister *say* about sin?" she persisted. "He was against it," said Cal.

So am I. It's just that my understanding of sin, and that of other progressives, often has more to do with the way that it manifests and perpetuates itself in social form. Individual moral failures and peccadilloes are one thing. The most deadly sins in our modern world are more often like those that Gandhi once listed: "wealth without work, pleasure without conscience, science without humanity, knowledge without character, politics without principle, commerce without morality, and worship without sacrifice." And all too often, as he knew, conventional religion is in the business of overlooking, justifying, or perpetuating those very things.

Progressives will never transform America's social sins, however, without an adequate doctrine of redemption or salvation. As G. K. Chesterton once observed, the United States is "a nation with the soul of a church." Contention over interpretation of the Bible has been a part of trying to mend its flaws since the beginning. Recently, however, liberals have been in danger of abandoning that attempt, walking away from it, and leaving the Bible and its interpretation to conservatives to use in paternalistic and oppressive ways.

We need a more mature understanding of our biblical heritage. Which is why many Buddhist teachers so often tell their best Western students to go home, reread the Bible, and develop a more mature understanding of the faith tradition of their culture.

Among my many volunteer responsibilities beyond my congregation, I serve as a trustee of the Massachusetts Bible Society. Now two hundred years old, it is one of the oldest groups devoted to helping promote pluralistic, progressive understandings of the Bible. Under the motto "One Book, Many Voices," the organization recently asked me to be one voice in a bicentennial video. Each person interviewed was to say something succinct about what everyone should know about the Bible. I first cited the progressive biblical scholar Walter Brueggemann, who once said, "I believe that we have become so jaded in the church—most particularly in the liberal church—that we have forgotten what has been entrusted to us. We have forgotten that the script entrusted to us is really an alternative and not an echo." It is a challenging, even subversive text. Then I said that I wish more people, even those who have *not* chosen the Bible as their spiritual guide, could see that you do not need to believe in anything "supernatural" to find in the Bible inspiration for both earth stewardship and social justice.

One has only to have eyes to see the super *within* nature. One has only to have ears for the breakthrough in history when the people of Israel, finding themselves somehow freed from bondage in Egypt, heard a Voice speaking to them through Moses, saying, in essence: "Don't ever treat anyone the way you were treated back there! Don't follow the Egyptians in worshipping the sun, the moon, or other parts of nature as divine, either. Worship only the mystery of creation and redemption. I am lifting up the lowly, bringing down the proud. I desire justice and peace." Nor is it hard to understand how, centuries later, when Israel itself had been conquered by one empire after another, under Roman rule, people were transformed and healed by hearing Jesus quote the prophet Isaiah in announcing his own mission: "The Spirit of the Lord is upon me, because he has anointed me to preach good news to the poor...to set at liberty those who are oppressed."

Many people yearn for a fresh, transforming encounter with the Bible, I find. When I do workshops on the topic, I often ask participants to write down stories, ideas, and passages from the Bible that they have long found troubling. Then I tell them that it would be a pity to leave their understanding of that text at the level of the Sunday school lesson, confirmation class, or oppressive sermon that left them turned off and alienated. Far too many people, I find, are still living at about age fourteen in relation to the scriptures. I tell them that my goal will be to offer them an alternative, more mature take on those very texts, even if it subverts their own long-held misunderstandings—because the Bible itself aims to turn the status quo and our prideful preconceptions upside down.

The great Jewish sage Martin Buber, who called himself a "biblical humanist," inspires me. Living under the Nazis, Buber was aware that Luther's translation of the Bible into German had carried some of the reformer's own anti-Judaism into the culture. So he was at work on a fresh translation of the Hebrew Bible into German when the Brownshirts came to his home, demanding that he surrender "all subversive literature." Buber handed them his Hebrew Bible, saying that its prophetic message was subversive of the very idolatry of blood and soil that their führer favored. Later he even dared to take that same stance into the new state of Israel.

Buber spoke of right relationships of mutuality and dialogue as "I and Thou" interactions. When it comes to the Bible, what I most hope is that people will have a fresh I and Thou experience, both with the text and with the Spirit behind it. Not that one can do more than set the necessary but not sufficient conditions for any such encounter. But simply removing some commonly held misconceptions about the Bible can often help. As Buber taught, we human beings all too often "mis-meet." We have mostly I-It encounters. We treat the Other—whether a human being or a sacred text—as just another object of our utility or convenience, perhaps of our wariness and resentment. Authentic meeting is rare. It takes place, he said, only on "a narrow ridge" between two dangers. One is the abyss of our own subjectivity, in which we are too preoccupied with our own feelings, experiences, and past pain to be truly present to the new encounter. The other is the slippery slope that opens up on the other side when we approach the encounter in arrogance, pretending that we already possess all the objective truth needed for a full understanding. Then I make a simple drawing that could be either Sinai or the mount where Jesus gave a sermon, or the roof of our meetinghouse. One slope I then label "literature" on the outside, and "subjective" on the inside. The other slope I label "history/science" on the outside, and "objective" on the inside. The "narrow ridge" is where the two lines meet. Just about where gutters would be on a roof plan, I draw two question marks, upside down, facing out. Then I say that many get caught in understandable, gut-level, but not very elevated, questions about the Bible.

Approaching it from the objective side of science and history, they keep sliding down to the question, "But did that *really* happen, and happen just the way it says here?" Obsessed with "objective truth," and often pretending to have it already, before trying to understand any other possibility, some people are like the man who volunteered to teach Sunday school but warned his minister that when it came to the parting of the Red Sea, he was going to tell the children about the theory he had seen on the History Channel: that there must have been a volcanic eruption in the Mediterranean, and then a tsunami. His minister replied, "And when you teach the story about

Jesus walking on the water, what are you going to suggest: that he found some rocks or sandbars to step out on?"

Sometimes we need to be reminded that all literature, sacred and profane alike, relies on metaphor. What is sometimes called "myth" is just a metaphor of narrative length. And unless we can imagine that those who followed Jesus had good reason to remember him as someone who, in a turbulent time, moved through storms with a buoyant faith and an inner calm that kept him above the waves, we may miss the inner, transforming meaning the story was intended to convey. The presence of mythic elements in a sacred text is no reason to stop trying to discern its applicable and higher meanings. Besides, behind a story elaborated into mythic form often lies something that really happened to real people.

Certainly those who try to read the Bible "as literature" alone meet other dangers. If you start from the beginning, reading alone, you will probably get bogged down in "the begats." In trying to read the Bible like a historical novel, it is easy to keep slipping down into the gut[ter]-level question, "But do I really *like* the lead character?" Again, this is understandable. In the early biblical legends, God can often seem like a textbook case of a rather bad parent—arbitrary, angry, and overreactive. He floods the whole world, for example, when the kids don't behave well. Later, God tells his chosen, favorite children to go destroy utterly the neighboring children.

Jack Miles, in his book *God: A Biography,* has the best response I know to this. Hang on; God gets better! In the course of interaction with God's people, the God of the Hebrew Bible shows important character development. By the time of the later prophets, such as the later Isaiah, God has rejected the holiness patterns of any particular earthly temple and is yearning for all of earth's children to come together in covenantal relationship, and to live in harmony not only with one another, but with the whole creation. "As a mother comforts her child, so will I comfort you," says God.

I have found that many sensitive souls can also have a hard time with the less-than-uplifting behavior of many of the human characters in the Hebrew Bible. Such people want every story to be one of moral exemplars, forgetting that one way we are taught to live at a higher plane is through cautionary tales. It is to the credit of Israel that it often tells both its own history and legends of its forebears from a higher, self-critical perspective. So rarely are even its greatest kings seen as entirely virtuous. The best of them is flawed. Their legends of the earliest humans and of distant forebears are similar. The stories about them are often about what *not* to do. In his book *The Genesis of Justice*, law professor Alan Dershowitz notes that many legends in Genesis seem to illustrate in negative ways the ideas that are in the Ten Commandments of the next scroll, Exodus.

Of course Americans hate rules, or being told what to do. But read the Ten Commandments this way: it is all simply experiential social wisdom. Take them in roughly reverse order. The final six have to do with loving one's neighbor. Don't covet, or steal, or lie, or commit adultery (which combines the above). Don't murder, or neglect your parents (especially if you want your own children to help you in later life). The first four may seem to be about duty to God. But in fact they are about not working all the time (as the pharaoh made his slaves work); about trusting God enough to take a day off to notice creation and practice spiritual re-creation. About not confusing God with any part of, or metaphor from, the created order—since this God is the creative, transformational One within all existence, including history. God then is not only the source of change, but the Creator behind a creation marked by change, chance, and choice. God is affected by what we do or leave undone and is changeless only in a steadfast intention to stay in relationship with us, intending *chesed* (loving-kindness), *mizpah* (justice), and *tzedakah* (righteousness).

Admittedly, the God of the Bible is often depicted, despite being beyond gender, in patriarchal terms. But we can also choose to see through this. Feminist interpretations of the Bible remind us that in nearly all ancient societies, women were rarely if ever given the chance to become literate. So it was the male scribes who took the wisdom stories derived from the real experiences of the people and recited around campfires and hearths, often by women, and turned them into scriptures that give the dominant role and authority to men. Feminist interpretation teaches us to read such texts with suspicion that the role and importance of women was downplayed in the process. Feminists contend that the more antifeminist scriptures should be read "against the grain."

For example, in some pastoral epistles of the early Christian movement, women are told to defer to their husbands and keep silent in church, and slaves are told to obey their masters. Why was this even necessary? Could it be because the same Christian movement recalled that among the early followers of Jesus, there had been a radical discipleship of equals? There is evidence of that. Even Paul spoke in the third chapter of Galatians of a fellowship in which there was "no longer Jew or Greek...no longer slave or free...no longer male and female," but only "children of God through faith," "one in Christ Jesus." So when, under pressure from the patriarchal norms of the time and Roman persecution, male authority figures in the early church advised groups to tell their women and slaves to conform to the *mores* of the world rather than being transformed by the renewing of their minds, we should perhaps not be too surprised, only disappointed. Sexism and fatalism do not represent the highest view in the scriptures, but rather a slide downward, from hope into conformity.

Perhaps all of this is quite familiar to you. *Mazel tov!* But to many people it is not. Progressive religion must reclaim its own evangelical mission: spreading the good news that *there is another way of reading the scriptures,* of interpreting the overarching canopy of our culture's Judeo-Christian heritage. It is past time for liberals of mainline Protestant background to embrace allies in this endeavor in Jewish, Catholic, Evangelical, Muslim, and even secular circles.

Admittedly, contention over how to read the biblical heritage is of long standing. Walter Brueggemann argues that you can see the conflict within the Hebrew Bible itself. The alternative voice he wants us to revive is the prophetic voice. It calls on us to be subversive of the status quo. (Look around you: wherever you are, if there is injustice, this is still Egypt!) It calls for liberation. It challenges idolatry. It refuses to worship Mammon. But he also admits that once a Jerusalem temple is built by King Solomon, there is an echo within it that is more about deference to hierarchy—provided it is ours. And more about purity, power, and pretensions to wisdom based on worldly ambitions. Often the prophetic tradition, down through Jesus, has to challenge the priestly when it neglects to keep the connection between ritual practices and ethical action.

To restore connections, we must often read texts cited by conservative opponents in either their literary or historical context. Or both. The hymn of praise for the Creation, for example, set as the preamble to the whole Bible, in Genesis 1, should be read as such—as a hymn, with seven stanzas and a refrain; and not as some form of science text! As Lutheran scholar Martin Marty once put it, teaching Genesis in biology classes makes about as much sense as trying to sing a page from a biology textbook at worship!

It may also help to realize how that hymn, as an assertion that creation is good and not a product of violence, probably entered the tradition as a result of the Babylonian exile, when priestly editors began to put the Hebrew Bible together. This work countered myths that privileged violence as creative, and the priests presented varied, sometimes clashing, versions of their own sacred story.

It may also help to realize that after the Exile, when God's people were reduced in numbers and trying to rebuild a covenantal community, the commandment to "increase and multiply" seemed newly important. Despite the earlier frequency of religious and ethnic intermarriage or of love like that between David and Jonathan, priestly prohibitions against both became inscribed in the scriptural tradition. Whether such ideas stand up today to prophetic imperatives to follow "justice, justice always," can still be argued. What is most important is that we not allow religious conservatives to pretend that the Bible belongs only to them. It belongs also to more prophetic progressives; the Bible itself says so.

Sometimes I wonder why we Americans seem to be able to read only non-Western scriptures from a higher, critical point of view. Even an isolate like J. D. Salinger, in his aptly titled story, "Raise High the Roof Beam, Carpenters," has the narrator declare toward the very end: "I've been reading a miscellany of Vedanta all day. Marriage partners are to serve each other. Elevate, help, teach, strengthen each other, but above all, serve. Raise their children honorably, lovingly, and with detachment. A child is a guest in the house, to be loved and respected—never possessed, since [s]he belongs to God. How wonderful, how sane, how beautifully difficult, and therefore true!"

So is much of the Bible—beautiful, difficult, and therefore true. Consider this text from the eighth chapter of Deuteronomy, which might well be read at American Thanksgiving tables, making that secular holiday more like a Passover seder: "When you have eaten your fill, and have built fine houses and lived in them, and when your herds and flocks have multiplied, and your silver and gold is multiplied, and all that you have is multiplied, then do not exalt yourself, forgetting the Lord your God, who brought you out of the land of Egypt, out of the house of slavery....Do not say to yourself, 'My power and the might of my own hand have gotten me this wealth.' But remember the Lord your God, for it is he who gives you power to get wealth, so that he may confirm his covenant that he swore to your ancestors."

I do not deny that the biblical heritage has contributed to a sense of America's exceptional place in the world, to a privileged sense of being God's holy, chosen people, and to a self-righteousness that should be subjected to critical scrutiny. But I do say that if we were to ask more often the prophetic questions that pervade the Bible, we might do better at what the Lord most requires of us: namely, doing justice, loving mercy, and walking humbly with our God.

One text in which that right relationship with God is explored, the sixth chapter of Micah, is intimately tied up with my sense of calling to progressive ministry. Here's why. During the Vietnam War, I heard Rabbi Abraham Joshua Heschel, of blessed memory, speak on that text, specifically the eighth verse, at an antiwar rally. He noted that Micah framed his statement in the form of a question, "What does the Lord require of you?" This is the role of prophets: not to provide all the answers, but to keep raising the vital, even if uncomfortable, questions. He warned those of us who were young (I was a senior in college) that sometime those threatened by prophetic questions attempt to silence the questioners, even by killing the prophets. When that happens, he said, echoing Buber, there is no solution to be found in the lives of isolated individuals, though one may hope that the spark of faith can be rekindled for them in their hour of need. The only solution is to be found in the lives of communities that attempt to live in the spirit of the prophets, keeping their questions alive while not pretending to have all the answers. On the night that Dr. King was killed later that year, I was sitting in a liberal church in which the words of Micah were displayed as a scriptural motto for a non-creedal congregation, and I wondered if something was not required of me by way of strengthening communities that keep alive the prophetic questions. I was wary of all easy and seemingly final answers. I still am.

Prophets are more likely to proclaim warning than comfort. But they live in hope. "Hope criticizes," said William Sloan Coffin. "Hopelessness rationalizes. Hope resists, hopelessness adapts." Today, says Walter Brueggemann, the task of progressive religionists is to be "practitioners of hope in a culture of despair. Faithful to the unseen, trans-human 'Source and Agent of newness, who is, in inscrutable ways, generative' within communities of faith and action," because "no one can fully hope alone." Such communities are where people learn again "to be what you want to see," as Gandhi put it.

The texts and traditions of others will be respected. But most such communities will gather beneath a sacred canopy that mediates between the realm above and the world around us. Let each be a courageous "community of interpretation that is emancipated, emancipatory, generative, and daring."

This is the promise of progressive religion in America I feel called to help keep. Taking refuge not from reality but within a house, a community, of hope.

PART FOUR

The Foundations

CHAPTER SEVEN

The Rocks Will Cry Out

Rebecca Parker

T he most ancient shrine described in the Bible was a rock.
As the story is told in Genesis, Jacob founded the shrine
because of a dream. Traveling alone, he fell asleep one night in
the mountains, with his head resting on a stone for his pillow.
Perhaps it was one of those bright nights when the stars are
thick and close, like a spangled quilt thrown over the earth. He
dreamed he saw a ladder connecting heaven and earth, with angels climbing up and down. "This is none other than the house
of God and the gate of heaven" he exclaimed when he woke.
He set up the stone to mark the place and named it Beth El—
the House of God. Another night, on another journey, Jacob
tossed and turned in fear that his brother, whom he'd wronged,
might kill him. An angel came in the darkness and fought him.
Jacob survived the fight but limped ever after, and he gained a
new name—Israel, which means "one who struggled with God
and lived."

The divine-human encounter is the rock on which our
theological house stands. At the heart of liberal theology is a

mysterious glimpse, a transforming struggle, with the oblique presence of God. "Theology" literally means "God-talk" and derives from *theos* (God) and *logos* (word). But talk of God is tricky business. The same Bible that tells of Jacob's marking stone also warns, "Make no graven images of God." God may be sighted by a sidewise glance, sensed in a dream, felt in a struggle, heard in the calm at the heart of a storm, or unveiled in a luminous epiphany. But the moment human beings think they know who God is and carve their conclusions in stone, images of God can become dangerous idols. In Jewish tradition, God is ultimately un-nameable, and some never pronounce the letters that spell out God's unspeakable name.

In liberal theology, at the core of the struggle with God is a restless awareness that human conclusions about God are always provisional, and any way of speaking about God may become an idol. This is why not everyone welcomes talk of God. God-talk has been used to hammer home expectations of obedience, to censure feelings and passions. It has been invoked to stifle intellectual inquiry and to reinforce oppression. For many people the word "God" stands for conceptions of the ultimate that have harmed life, sanctioned unjust systems, or propelled people to take horrific actions "in the name of God."

"If this is God," black religious humanist William R. Jones commented in a conversation considering white Christianity's standard concepts of God, "he is my enemy. My sincere obligation is to fight him." Jones's book *Is God a White Racist?* contends that images of God have functioned to justify slavery and lynching rather than to alleviate black suffering. In *Facing the Abusive God*, Jewish theologian David Blumenthal reflects that for many Jews it became impossible to accept the existence of God after the genocide of World War II. If God would stand by in silence as God's people were gassed by the millions, God either was unspeakably cruel, powerless, absent, or nonexistent. Rabbi Blumenthal recovers the significance of theology by blessing the act of fighting with God as the only means by which human dignity can be asserted in the aftermath of the Holocaust.

For the past two hundred years, theologians have been wrestling with theism—deconstructing image after image of God that has functioned idolatrously and oppressively. Progressive theology has dethroned God as king, undone God the father, exposed the fallacy of God as white, as male, as straight, as able-bodied, as "Unmoved Mover," and more. As early as the 1960s, theologians were announcing the death of God. In the name of justice and liberation, theologians themselves have brought about God's demise and conducted the funeral.

Recently, books arguing for atheism have been high on the best-seller charts, but as Chris Hedges points out in his countering book, *I Don't Believe in Atheists,* the new atheists mirror the fundamentalist habits of mind they rail against, and they betray a shocking ignorance of the serious cross-examination of God that has been under way for the past two centuries—as an act of faith by people of faith. Moreover, their Islamophobic rants can be even less attractive than their bitterness against Christianity and Judaism. Thoughtful people of many faiths hold that if there is a God, God must be worthy of our devotion—not an enemy of what is good in us and not the divine authorizer for acts of injustice, terror, and oppression. The nineteenth-century Unitarian Theodore Parker put it well: the goodness of God is manifest in that God has given humanity the power to judge God.

Liberal theological judgments of God began early in the nineteenth century in reaction to the oppressive, terrifying image of God as the all-powerful controller of humanity's destiny. Elizabeth Cady Stanton, who reports being frightened by the preaching she heard in her childhood, was liberated by her encounter with the emerging liberal theology of her day. Preachers such as William Ellery Channing pictured God as a loving father rather than as an all-powerful, condemning king. Cady Stanton embraced the new theology, which placed ideas about God on a new foundation. Rather than submitting to established doctrine, human beings could come to know God from observation of the world and contemplation of human experience. Building on a new sense of God, she became an activist to promote a new sense of women's power and possibilities in the world.

Channing affirmed, "The creation is a birth and shining forth of the Divine Mind, a work through which his spirit breathes." Because God was in all things, the revelation of God's nature could be discerned in "everything, from the frail flower to the everlasting stars." Human life itself, above all, was for Channing a source of knowledge of God, since every human being reflects the image of God:

> Whence do we derive our knowledge of the attributes and perfections which constitute the Supreme Being?...We derive them from our own souls....The idea of God, sublime and awful as it is, is the idea of our own spiritual nature, purified and enlarged to infinity....God is another name for human intelligence raised above all error and imperfection....We see God around us, because he dwells within us.

Once human experience becomes a starting point for imagining God, it becomes important to ask *whose* human experience is authoritative, and *what* experiences? The plot thickens even further when essentialist notions of universal "human nature" give way to complex and particularized understandings of gender, gender expression, race, culture, and class as socially and historically constructed. Early in the twentieth century, Charlotte Perkins Gilman in *His Religion and Hers* advanced a feminist critique and reimagining of God. Gilman argued that had women's experience of birth-giving been the source of religion instead of men's experience of hunting and killing, then a very different religion would result. She wrote in 1923:

> Birth based religion…would tell no story of old sins, of anguish and despair, of passionate pleading for forgiveness for the mischief we have made, but would offer always the sunrise of fresh hope: "Here is a new baby. Begin again!" To the mother comes the apprehension of God as something coming; she sees [God's] work, the newborn child, as visibly unfinished and calling for continuous service.…As the thought of God slowly unfolded in the mind of woman, that great Power would have been apprehended as the Life-giver, the Teacher, the Provider, the Protector—not the proud, angry, jealous, vengeful deity men have imagined. She would have seen a God of Service, not a God of Battles.

In the early 1970s, Mary Daly's *Beyond God the Father* decisively undid male images of God—linking such images directly to the subjugation of women's experience and intellect. In the decades that followed, women's theological work dismantled idols and resurrected images that affirm women's cultural identities and bodies. This work has shaken the foundations of established religion. Women who claimed the authority to reimagine God met with backlash. Cultural investment in God the father, king, and judge retains powerful support. The 1990s Reimagining Conference—an international gathering of women in religion where the voices and theologies of women of color were in the lead—was fiercely opposed by established church leaders and people on the political right. The Institute on Religion and Democracy, which is funded by secular, right-wing political and economic interests, mounted a concerted effort to condemn the conference organizers and leaders. As a result of that organization's pressure, a number of high-ranking women in major American Protestant denominations were fired. Feminist theologians stood up to the hostility. Rita Nakashima Brock, who had given one of the major addresses at the Reimagining Conference, appeared on a national news program and defended the rights of women to do theology in our own voices.

How people speak of God has profound public significance. To justify their actions, those who want to maintain that "America" is God's chosen nation and has the right to destroy evildoers with God's blessing need the old image of God as a sovereign, all-powerful father and warrior. Those who struggle for room to breathe, for freedom from oppression, for dignity and the right to exist, for wholeness and integrity, and for an end to war, welcome the death of this God.

Protest against unworthy images of God is a deeply religious act. In the biblical story of Job, Job shakes his fist at a concept of God which conveniently blessed those doing well and cursed those in pain. Job abandoned the image of God held by his friends who told him his suffering meant God was punishing him for his sins. He interrogated God, face to face. When he did, the cosmos opened. The whirlwind confronted him—a swirl of chaos and creativity. In the midst of the stormy blast, his understanding of God's nature was transformed.

"Languaging the whirlwind" is how theologian Langdon Gilkey characterized the task of theology following the 1960s death-of-God movements. Theology must speak from the spaces of chaos and creativity that emerge when stone-cold, idolatrous images of God have been dismantled by the force of a righteous critique. It is in those spaces that fresh discoveries arise and new understanding of how it may be possible to speak of God come. In the space of God's absence, a new encounter with divine presence may be experienced—an encounter from outside or the underside.

The characters in Alice Walker's novel *The Color Purple* speak of the necessity of clearing away the internalized oppressor before one can come to a life-giving sense of God. Celie writes to Nettie, "The God I been praying and writing to is a man. And act just like all the other mens I know. Trifling, forgetful and lowdown." Her friend Shug responds, "Ain't no way to read the bible and not think God white....When I found out I thought God was white, and a man, I lost interest....You have to git man off your eyeball, before you can see anything a'tall." Shug abandoned the image of God as an old white man in the clouds and tells Celie she has come to see God as It, as everything, as the connectedness among all things, as the lover of everything we love, including sexual pleasure. God seeks our attention, admiration, and love through life's beauty, diversity, and creativity—trees, people, a field blooming in the color purple. Shug says, "It always making little surprises and springing them on us when we least expect."

A dream I had as a young minister showed me how difficult it can be to come to a new sense of God. In the dream, I am walking along a city street on a winter afternoon. The sidewalk is covered with gray slush, and passing cars and trucks spray me with dirty water as they charge through puddles and ice. I feel anxious and unprotected, so I turn down a narrow, dingy alley to escape the mess. Barely able to see, I make out in the dim light that in every doorway there are homeless people in tattered clothes and that they all have lonely eyes and are shivering. One by one they step out of their doorways and walk behind me until there is a small crowd. I sense their need and am frightened by their silence. Suddenly, the alleyway comes to a dead end at a brick wall with a door in it. I must either go through the door or turn around and go back through the crowd of suffering humanity. Both options frighten me. I choose the door, opening it and stepping through quickly. The door swings shut behind me, locked. In the claustrophobic darkness, a faint green light like an illuminated watch dial reveals the presence of an imposing person. I am terrified. I immediately see that the person wears a crown on which is written "king of the bums." The leader of the destitute is mute, but the green light is coming from the sign he holds. Letters spell out a message: "God is so tender, sometimes she is called Green."

The sense of God as tender, as fragile as a new shoot of green life, has stayed with me. So too has the awareness that coming to such a sensibility often happens when one takes a turn that requires one to face into suffering. Perhaps the dream was a forecast of the journey I would have to make into the abandoned and mute part of myself, the outcast realms of my own being—the neighborhood in my own soul that I was afraid to visit at night. Perhaps it also indicated that awareness of God's presence emerges from a seed of life present in difficult circumstances, in human beings experiencing homelessness and lack of adequate food or clean water who find ways to establish sustaining ties of human community. "What if God is our baby to bear?" Annie Dillard asks in *Holy the Firm.* What if the new life, the tender existence of the divine, enters the world through places where life is at risk and people must come together to create ways to tend life with care so it will survive?

In Proverbs of Ashes, Rita Nakashima Brock and I tell stories from our lives and the lives of those we have known and worked with, who had to struggle through oppressive theologies before coming to a new sense of God. We testify that facing into human suffering is necessary and that in communities of justice and compassion, God's presence can be manifest as people offer loving presence to one another. Such presence heals and transforms, and it elicits surprising revelations of life's resilience and grace. After long struggle, Rita writes:

This is how I can speak of God: a presence gradually unfolded by life in its richness and tragedies, its devastating
losses and its abundance: a power calling us into a fullness
of living, a passion for life, for good and ill: an unquench-
able fire at the core of life, glimpsed in light and shadows.

Is it reasonable to believe in God? The question "Does God
exist?" can be a metallic, hard-edged question about what is
factually true. As if scientists in a glistening clean lab, peering
through microscopes, could settle the matter. Is there evidence?
But the question "Does God exist?" arises in another way—not
as a cool inquiry into the nature of ultimate reality. It arises in
the messy, painful dead ends, on the cold winter afternoons
where life is exposed to the raw elements. It arises among the
communities of those lacking bare necessities. It arises among
the lonely, the hungry, the frightened, and those without voice.
In such settings, the question is not about metaphors or about
rational arguments. It is more elemental. It is a question borne
in the suffering souls of human beings, and its meaning is a
cry for hope. Is there any help for pain? Is there anything that
will spring green from this bitter winter, with its dirty ice and
slush? Is there any hope for the disempowered and silenced?
The abandoned? And when everything human fails, and nothing that is within the power of human beings to do can be
done, what then? *Does God exist?* Is there a source of healing
and transformation that will bring about justice in heaven or
on earth?

The fundamental question then is an *existential* question,
not merely an intellectual exercise. Do you believe in God? is a
relatively meaningless question, compared to the inquiry of the
heart: is there reason to trust that there is any help available?
And believing in the possibility of God is only a tentative first
step. Beyond that is the matter of trusting that there is some-

thing or someone beyond us that desires that we be free, whole, and joyful; that desires the thriving of life in its beautiful diversity and abundance; and that has the power, in connection with us, to heal, transform, liberate and enliven our existence.

The answer to this question cannot be coerced. Religious tradition can show a path and give some clues, but when a person or a community is up against a wall, facing a dead end in the alley, tradition at best serves as a nudge to take the next step—whether it is to try the closed door or turn to face into suffering humanity with courage—or both. Revelation comes to those who are radically hospitable to what they do not know. The choice to take the next step is an act of holy curiosity. It could also be called an act of faith. To those who act on faith, to those who move in the midst of mystery and silence, even when trembling and afraid, the face of God sometimes appears. New ways of speaking of God arise from the luminous dark. Revelation is not sealed. In the course of our struggles for justice, one of the strange others we may meet is a tender shoot of green, in response to which some of us will breathe the word *God.*

"The final appeal is to intuition," writes mathematician and philosopher Alfred North Whitehead. He means that, finally, whether or not one has faith in God requires an intuition about the nature of things. But for Whitehead, intuition is firmly grounded in life. It is the result of an accumulation of experience and observation that operates even before conscious deliberation. The full body of our experience, like a deep ocean, sometimes casts up onto the shore of consciousness a conclusion that arrives like a translucent agate resting in the glistening sand. If we are watching closely as we walk, we can see it. This is how the intuition that God exists comes for some. It is the only thing that makes sense of all that is experienced and observed—not only of tragedy and loss but also of beauty and surprise.

Writing early in the twentieth century, Whitehead worked out a profound concept of the nature of God. His cosmological work *Process and Reality* has provided the basis for subsequent generations of theologians to reimagine God. Intuition may have been his final court of appeal, but Whitehead began with a disciplined consideration of the implications of post-Newtonian physics. Up until the birth of relativity theory and quantum physics, Western science conceived of the "stuff" of reality as tiny bits of hard matter that built up into structures—from atoms to rocks, from molecules to trees and lizards and human beings. At its foundation, the "real world" was formed from an aggregation of atoms, just as the foundation of the Needham meetinghouse was built of stones mortared together. In keeping with this scientific worldview, God's reality was imagined to itself be like that of an ordinary rock: solid, unfeeling, unchanging, able to affect other things, but not itself affected. Classical theism described God's nature as omnipotent, impassable, and eternal.

But with the dawn of post-Newtonian physics, the nature of ultimate reality dematerialized. The building blocks of the universe turn out not to be tiny bits of hard matter, but tiny activities. Science now reveals to us a world that is relational, interactive, codeterminate, chaotic, intermittent, and ever changing. Whitehead saw that the new scientific worldview required a reconsideration of basic categories in Western philosophy. The Cartesian dualisms of mind and matter, subject and object, spirit and flesh no longer held firm. There was no such thing as matter uninhabited by spirit, subjects that endure through time as containers to hold objects. These categories collapsed, and, with them, the solid, impassive God of classical theism dissolved.

Rocks are not what they used to be. Now we understand that inside a stone, there is a vibrating dance of activity. From the perspective of process theology, God the Supreme Being can be called "a rock" as the psalmist says, but a rock is an *activity*, not a steady state: it is an aggregate of motion. All beings, Whitehead noted, are actually events-in-process. In Whitehead's philosophy, the being-becoming event begins with feeling all other events—receiving and being affected by the vast network of all existence. It advances to an integration of everything into a felt unity that manifests its subjective aim. With its aim instantiated, the event passes from immediacy and becomes an object to be felt by the new crop of events arising in the next moment. Everything that exists, exists as an instance of this process—a process that is relational, ongoing, creative, emergent, and grounded in all that has been.

God, for process theology, is an event-in-process like all others—not a metaphysical exception, but part and parcel of the nature of reality. God's being is distinctive not in kind but in quality. God is supreme in sensitivity—feeling everything with fullness. God is supreme in integration—holding everything with "care that nothing be lost," Whitehead says. God is supreme in love, sympathy, and joy. God's aim—as the world's religious wisdom traditions witness—is for life to flourish, justice to be done, compassion to be expressed, beauty to manifest, and peace to be accomplished here and now.

God's feeling for the plenitude of existence evolves moment by moment, in creative response to all that is happening. How God feels is available for every event-in-process to feel—from the tiniest beat in the rhythm of an atom to the successive integrative moments that constitute each human being's soul. God provides the world with an ever-fresh and ever-particular embrace of loving compassion here and now, and a pulse of desire for the best that could come into being in the future.

From the heart of God, alluring guidance flows into the world. God's imagination and longing, felt by every event-in-process, invites each particular thing to its potential part in the advance of peace, joy, healing, beauty, zest—abundant life. Whether God's "initial aim"—Whitehead's term for God's particular guidance to each being—is manifest depends on the decision of each being, which is free to choose to align with the divinely proposed possibilities as a cocreator with God.

Process theology's reconceptualization of God fits well with the many liberation movements in theology that have deconstructed God-talk, protesting images of God that sanction oppression and violence. It resonates with biblical understandings of God's active, creative presence in nature and history—which should not be divided into separate realities. It focuses on immediacy, spontaneity, and relationality similarly to Taoism and to Buddhist traditions and practices. And it presents God as the constant instigator of needed transformation in the world. Where there is oppression, injustice, abuse, or neglect, God's creative response offers new possibilities to all beings, luring them toward decisions and actions that will advance healing, liberation, and justice. The divine possibilities are more than abstract ideals—dreams of what should be. They come to the world as specific proposals for specific situations. Immediate, contextual, and multisided, God's love for life takes all sides—oppressor and oppressed—and proposes a way of peace and justice tailored to the concrete dilemmas and opportunities present for each.

Rooted in science, reason, and intuition, process theology provides a way of understanding the existence of God that progressive theology can embrace in the twenty-first century. This is not a despotic monarch, ruling through coercion and threat, sanctifying violence. This is not an unchanging, eternal reality from which the imperfect can be condemned. This is not merely a metaphor, but an actual presence, alive and afoot in the cosmos, an upholding and sheltering presence that receives and feels everything that happens with compassion and justice, offering the world back to itself, in every moment, with a fresh impulse to manifest the values of beauty, peace, vitality, and liberation. God is everlastingly emergent, alive, responsive, creative, at one with the chaotic, messy universe we live in.

Whitehead calls God "the fellow sufferer who understands," "the poet of the world," and the lure toward peace. Does this God exist? My intuition says yes. Yours may say no. However the question is answered, it is provisional. The very rocks cry out to tell us that stillness is an illusion and that motion is the reality. God's beauty shimmers, dances, melts, and flows. The angels circle up and down on Jacob's ladder. We set up marking stones at the epiphany places and build our theological houses. Meanwhile, God invites us to open the door and cross the threshold into mystery.

CHAPTER EIGHT

The Changing of the Foundations

John Buehrens

God changes.

There, I've said it. It's the central affirmation, I believe, of progressive theology. Some conservatives may call it "heresy." I can understand that. Many of us were raised with an opposite assertion. We sang great hymns saying, "Change and decay in all around I see: O Thou who changest not, abide with me." So let me say that I also believe that God *does* abide, and endures, even as mortals, civilizations, and the ages pass.

In his book *Love and Death*, written while he was dealing with terminal cancer, my dear friend and colleague Forrest Church repeated a longtime assertion: "God is not God's name." That is, "God" is only the word that we mortals in Western culture have for a reality far more profound and connective than any of our various inherited images of the holy. God is a reality, Forrest says, "present in each, yet greater than all." This reality is relational. So how could God *not* change? Surely *we* change. History changes. The universe itself changes.

The history of theology is all about changing human conceptions of the divine. Consider Robert Wright's book *The Evolution of God*. Or simply go back to the Bible. There the relational nature of God, with God affected and changed by what we do or leave undone, is far clearer than in philosophical theologies later on. Because ever since Jerusalem met Athens, and the followers of philosophy met the Bible, theology in the West has tried to pay God abstract, static, philosophical, and metaphysical compliments. In the process, it made the "God" of Western theism not only *omnipresent*, but also *omniscient, omnipotent*, and, perhaps worst of all, *impassive*.

That last term translates as "unaffected and unchanged"— by us, by our human actions, failures, or sufferings. There may be ways to reinterpret these terms in ways that are both spiritually useful and intellectually coherent. But for many people, the God of such classical theism has only receded further and further away—up and out, away from the Creation, from history, and from human living itself, into a distant, transcendent, and increasingly irrelevant space beyond all time.

But before we say goodbye to God entirely, too easily, some reconstruction of history may be in order. This problem in theology was named as long ago as the 1500s. An Italian biblical scholar called Faustus Socinus, a leader in the radical wing of the Reformation in Poland, said that God is neither static nor impassive. He thought both ideas contradicted scripture—making him, according to twentieth-century American philosopher Charles Hartshorne, perhaps the first "process theologian." Hartshorne, who influenced both Rebecca Parker and me, joined Alfred North Whitehead in creating a process view of all reality, one adequate to what modern physical science has now taught us.

Everything is in process. Even the seemingly solid bedrock of earth has gone through enormous changes since it was star-stuff, then magma. Nor is reality quite as the ancients saw it:

changing combinations of earth, fire, water, and air (or spirit). Nor is it made up chiefly of mass and space, as in Newtonian physics. What seem to us to be "things" are just packets of energy, related for a time. They are events, actual occasions. So are we. Any metaphysics or theology for today must reflect that reality.

All creation is an event. Religiously, it is a "theophany"— manifesting the divine. Relational creativity is pervasive. So when we ask, as humans often do, "Where is God?" the answer is that God is in all things, yet not exhausted by them. This is not pantheism. Rather, philosophers call it "pan*en*theism." God is present *in* all things, but also greater than all. God is never truly absent. Often it is *we* who are absent, taught Martin Buber. Too often we are self-involved, failing to notice. Or worse, we are actively destroying our connection with our fellow human beings and with the holy. "We are here to abet creation and to witness to it, to notice each other's beautiful face and complex nature," declares Annie Dillard, "so that creation need not play to an empty house."

But a changing God can be hard to recognize. We go looking for something godlike but ultimately idolatrous, and we do so in all the wrong places. How we go out looking changes as well. Changes in culture and circumstance change even the most seemingly solid ground of our understanding and search. The Needham meetinghouse, where I preach most Sundays, seems to testify to this truth. Now it rests upon a recently renovated foundation, restored for the twenty-first century. But a quick review of our parish history discloses that new foundations have been laid under our house of hope and worship several times before. In fact, the meetinghouse had new foundations laid in 1720, 1774, 1836, 1879 (when the whole building was moved), 1922, and then, before the 2008 renovation, around sixty years ago, in 1948.

Liberal theologian Paul Tillich was then preaching his sermons speaking of God as "the Ground of Being." These became a book called *The Shaking of the Foundations*. But religious history suggests that we only touch any absolute ground of being indirectly, through stones quarried locally, then very humanly mortared together. We can easily come to believe that our human constructions are absolute and eternal, but they are temporary structures, habitations for the time being. And we can forget that God too is changing. The changing foundations of our House for Hope correspond roughly to successive new eras in the history of liberal theology in America as a whole.

The first foundation of the Needham meetinghouse was simple Puritan fieldstone. No doubt the first minister, Jonathan Townsend, thought the foundation of his preaching was gathered from scripture. "Where were *you* when I laid the foundations of the earth?" God inquires of Job. Somewhat later, in First Corinthians, Paul asserts, "For other foundation no man can lay than that which is laid, which is Jesus Christ."

When the meetinghouse burned in 1773, after a six-year quarrel about moving it, the next minister and the parish majority rebuilt on the same site but laid a new foundation. Their text was from Psalm 11: "If the foundations be destroyed, what can the righteous do?" Times were changing, however. God had also changed, at least in human perception. "Common Sense" theology had taken over. The distant clockmaker God of Newton's universe, dominant during the eighteenth century, had failed to move human hearts. One response was the very subjective idealism of philosophic cleric Bishop Berkeley. God or reality exists only in the minds of perceivers. Samuel Johnson supposedly refuted the good bishop by just kicking a rock. Another was the atheistic naturalism of David Hume: rocks *are* rocks. Common Sense theology challenged both. "Self-evident" to humans with common sense, said this view, were not only Nature, but also Nature's God and even certain human "inalienable rights," as the Declaration of Independence put it.

Among these were individual rights of conscience. The next Needham minister, the Reverend Stephen Palmer, noting increasing diversity of theological opinion in his flock, wrote: "Every man will have a creed of his own. I have mine; but I have no right to impose it upon others, nor have others any right to impose theirs upon me. I have never viewed my opinions to be such mountains as a different faith cannot remove, nor have I ever believed myself to be infallible. He who thinks he has no more light to receive, has seen but little; and he who is not open to conviction, is in bondage to himself."

Palmer had a well-grounded theology; one of civic democracy and of good morals. Like many in his era, he felt that "God's firm foundation stands, bearing this inscription: 'The Lord knows those who are his,' and 'Let everyone who calls on the name of the Lord turn away from wickedness.'" But by the time the foundation was laid under the third meetinghouse in 1836, there was a moral crisis in American democracy concerning the institution of slavery. The founders of the American Republic wrote slavery into the Constitution, the compact between the states. What moral ground was there to challenge such a foundational agreement?

William Ellery Channing was the leader of liberal religious thought in that era. *The Making of American Liberal Theology*, Gary Dorrien's great three-volume history, starts with Channing. Like Palmer, he wanted the kind of free, universal church from which "no man can be excommunicated but by himself, by the death of goodness in his own breast"—not by any failure to meet a merely abstract, creedal, theological test. Channing grew up in Newport, Rhode Island. When he was a boy, slaves were still being unloaded on the docks there, part of the "triangular trade" that had made Newport rich. Later, after college but before ordination, he saw slavery down in Virginia when he worked as a tutor on a plantation. Settled as a pastor in Boston to an affluent congregation including merchants and cotton-mill owners, Channing began to realize how he and his flock had also profited from exploiting slaves. Never a radical by temperament, he still had a radical insight at the core of his liberalism. Dan McKanan, in his study *Identifying the Image of God: Radical Christians and Nonviolent Power in the Antebellum United States,* describes the change in theology this way. Early Puritan theology had been all about God as sovereign, terrible, and distant. Postrevolutionary New England religion restored the ancient theology of the *imago dei*—the image of God found in every human being. In an 1828 sermon, "Likeness to God," Channing declared, "We approach the Creator by every right exertion of powers...[given] us. Whenever we invigorate the understanding by honestly and resolutely seeking truth...whenever we invigorate the conscience by following it...or encounter peril or scorn with moral courage...whenever we receive a blessing gratefully, perform a disinterested deed; whenever we lift up the heart in true adoration...think, speak, or act with moral energy...then the divinity is growing within us."

He summarized by saying, "God becomes...real...to us in proportion as the divine is unfolded within us."

This is sound doctrine. Today's Episcopal Church, in its *Book of Common Prayer,* asks what it means to be made in God's image. Then it answers: "It means that we are *free* to make choices: to love, to create, to reason, and to live in harmony with creation and with God" (emphasis added). It could have also added, "and with one another." But if God is free, God changes.

Channing's *imago dei* theology not only laid the groundwork for abolishing slavery. Through followers such as Ralph Waldo Emerson, who had Channing as a mentor, it also opened the way for grounding religion itself in something wider and deeper than only the biblical heritage—in a personal yet universal intuition of a spiritual and moral foundation to all authentic human living called "Transcendentalism."

Among the leaders of the Transcendentalists was the eloquent Boston minister Theodore Parker, who preached to thousands and whose sermons were widely reprinted. They contained phrases later associated with others who changed the very grounding of American spiritual life. When Lincoln spoke at the Gettysburg burial ground about "government of the people, by the people, and for the people," he paraphrased Parker. When Martin Luther King Jr. said that "the moral arc of the universe is long, but it bends toward justice," he was paraphrasing Parker. A grandson of Captain John Parker, who led the Minutemen at Lexington, Theodore Parker came to feel that the Constitution, in accepting slavery, was so immoral that a "second American Revolution" was needed, especially after the Fugitive Slave Act was included in the Great Compromise of 1850. Whereas Emerson simply wrote in his journal, "This filthy enactment...I will not obey it, by God!" Parker actually hid fugitive slaves in his house and among his congregation. He kept a pistol handy in case a federal marshal came. Before John Brown tried raising a slave insurrection, Parker had raised money to aid his efforts.

By 1850, Transcendentalism had even come to rural Needham's pulpit and parsonage. The Reverend Charles Dall had been a minister-at-large to the poor in several eastern cities. Influenced by his wife, Caroline Healey Dall, who had been listening to Theodore Parker, Dall began to challenge the foundations of the simple, traditional faith of many in his flock. Meanwhile Caroline, only twenty-two, shocked local farmers by publishing a book of her own—with essays condemning the war against Mexico, supporting the abolition of slavery, and, most revolutionary of all, in "Sisterhood," advocating full and equal rights for women. Some said that Caroline cost her husband his pastorate. Others said he could have lost it quite easily all by himself! In any case, there were soon groups in Needham founding congregations set on more conservative principles: for Baptists, for Trinitarian and Evangelical Congregationalists, and for Methodists.

After the Civil War, the foundations of liberal religion in America changed again. In Needham, First Parish moved its meetinghouse nearer the railhead and town center. The new foundation was laid there in 1879. Industrialization was one source of change. Another was new thinking about God and evolution. "How do we cooperate with God, change, and more fully follow Jesus in laying the foundation for the kingdom of God here amid these new conditions?" liberal Christians asked. The "New Thought of God" believed that a God grounded in evolution itself would bring things around right.

Then came World War I. Millions of young soldiers died in trench warfare. The easy comfort of a God at work for good in natural processes crumbled. The postwar period was a time of great uneasiness. In England, workers came to realize that their churches were funded by patrons who had profited from war industries. On the continent, masses in defeated nations turned toward idolatrous forms of "die for your country" ideology. Totalitarian hatred challenged democratic practice. Nor did America escape entirely.

In 1920s America, Christian fundamentalists and religious modernists divided. The Scopes "monkey" trial was the epitome of the split. The Ku Klux Klan recruited almost 15 percent of American Protestants. Even in the Boston area, the Klan took over a previously liberal Universalist congregation. Humanists announced "the end of theism." Meanwhile, in Needham, the congregation put a new foundation under the meetinghouse, around a new lower hall, for church suppers and theatrical performances. Serious progressive theologians such as Reinhold Niebuhr tried to warn that religious liberals were whistling in the dark, talking about their ideals up on high while ignoring the rising tide of totalitarianism and, in the depths of the Depression, merely entertaining one another. Such progressive realism was not popular, however.

After World War II, God changed again. Liberal religion in America flowed in at least three streams. Niebuhr and Tillich were sometimes called "neo-orthodox," but were really offering a liberal theological response to fundamentalism. A second stream seemed more radical. Renouncing most forms of God-talk entirely, religious humanism presented itself as a new, more solid basis of inclusive community. But the broadest stream was simply the one that flowed toward the suburbs. Progressive theologians began to fret about what they called the growing middle-class "suburban captivity of the church."

True to its liberal traditions, First Parish in Needham fed on the latter two streams. The foundations for a Sunday school wing were laid as the congregation grew. Its ministers were religious humanists. The phrase "under God" may have been added to the U.S. Pledge of Allegiance. But it was more to reject "atheistic communism" than to critique American society from any higher perspective. When the civil rights movement came, and Dr. King called upon the clergy of America to come to Selma, Alabama, the humanist minister in Needham responded. So did many others. One religious humanist, the Reverend James Reeb, was even killed there.

But after the civil rights movement of the 1960s, the very foundations of American society and progressive religious thought again seemed to change. Black nationalism, feminism, postcolonialism, the new immigration, the gay rights movement—each contributed multiple forms of progressive, liberation theology. To some critics, each also seemed to claim to be the cornerstone. Even progressive theologian Harvey Cox worried about what held the various forms of liberation theology together, and whether the mutual critique and dialogue among them was not allowing conservative religion to claim a larger place on public platforms by seeming more cohesive. Using "wedge issues" including abortion, homosexuality, and Cold War politics to divide liberals, conservatives succeeded in bringing together such traditional rivals as Protestant evangelicals and the Catholic hierarchy.

Meanwhile, within progressive religion there have been steady efforts to realize that liberation cries of people of color, women, and sexual minorities are really one cry—for dignity in diversity and release from oppression. Jesus himself said that if his followers were silent, the very stones would cry out. What liberation theology has shown is that all theology can be quarried only from the ground of personal and communal experience. And those stones *do* cry out, even in the face of God's seeming silence or that of those in power above.

Unspeakable suffering, after all, can challenge the very foundations of faith. "Where is God?" Elie Wiesel, as a child in a Nazi death camp, heard a fellow Jew ask that question as another boy was being executed. The answer came from deep within him: "Here he is; He is hanging on this gallows." For a decade following, Wiesel kept silent. He knew that for many, God had died, or turned to stone; and that there are risks in breaking the silence about God. Those who speak for or to their fellow sufferers about God emerging beyond such devastations have been challenged not to imply that God can be found only in and through experiences of suffering, violence, and death, but in the ongoing goodness of life. But others refused to keep theological silence. They did so, in Abraham Heschel's words, "out of compassion for God," the fellow sufferer.

Process theology speaks about a God who is no guarantor

of a static order of being, but who is profoundly affected and changed by what we human beings do to one another and to the creation. This is a God of unending creativity who is not dead at all, but who rises in human hearts beyond the grief and loss that God shares with us. A God who, in Alfred North Whitehead's words, is "the fellow sufferer who understands." Progressive theology that matters, however, will not be about metaphysical process alone. It will be integrated with the experiences of suffering and liberation of real individuals and communities. It will find its foundations in a profoundly relational view of reality—one that satisfies both the insights of modern science and that attends to the varied experiences of God's children.

"Come to him, a living stone, though rejected by mortals yet chosen and precious in God's sight and, like living stones, let yourselves be built into a spiritual house," says the First Epistle of Peter. The challenge is to not let our hearts be turned to stone by tragedy but to meld with one another in a reconstruction of faith and love.

Conservative theology often presents God as immutable, as having formed an unchangeable will for all that occurs. I can never agree. I'm reminded of one of my mentors in progressive theology, the late William Sloan Coffin, who lost a beloved son in a car accident. When a pious parishioner paid a condolence call, sighing, "Sometimes I just can't understand the will of God," Bill let loose. "I'll say you can't!" he yelled. It wasn't God's will that the road was unlighted, that the car needed new windshield wipers, or that his son had probably had one beer too many. "God's heart was the first to break," he sobbed.

I can't lay out here a full outline of the theology needed now to rebuild the foundation under our shared house of hope. One that integrates a sense of the changing dynamics of underlying and ultimate Reality with the shaking and changing of the human-built foundations that still oppress so many of God's children. What I can recount is a story from my experience as the minister of an old yet revitalized congregation.

There is a little girl in my parish named Gwen. She is almost seven. That she has survived even to this age is something of a human and medical miracle. As I often tell people, one of the conditions on which we seem to have life, and the chance for freedom, change, and creativity, is that things can also go randomly, radically wrong. Gwen has a little-understood genetic illness, mitochondrial disease. There is something wrong with the parts of her cells that produce energy. Many children have probably died of this problem. No one knew until quite recently how to recognize it. There is still little to be done except treat symptoms, which are different in each child.

Gwen is beautiful. And at times she seems perfectly bouncy and normal in every way. She sings in our children's choir with her older sister. And then her body betrays her—most recently, by allowing the bacteria in her gut to migrate into her bloodstream. Last year, Gwen was in a pediatric intensive-care unit so often that everyone lost count of the days. Then she nearly died. Her parents said to her, "We're not ready for you to go." And she didn't. But she may still. We all will in time.

Gwen has two moms. That has absolutely nothing to do with her illness. But when she was little, and her doctors could not understand what was wrong with her, her moms were subjected to the excruciating experience of being accused of *causing* Gwen's illness—of seeking attention through her, of "Munchausen by proxy syndrome." Such cruel distrust can literally turn you to stone. Or else it can turn you toward others, in complete openness and honest, human vulnerability. Gwen's moms chose the latter path. They moved to Needham to be closer to a team of doctors at one of Boston's world-famous hospitals—a team who trusted them and whom they came to trust in return. Recently, Gwen got a multiorgan transplant: new stomach, intestine, liver, pancreas, and spleen. Thank God.

Neither of Gwen's two moms would use much traditional theological language. Sue considers herself a Buddhist. When she can't maintain her own composure in the face of Gwen's pain, which is extreme at times, Sue has been known to say, "My inner Buddhist has run away." Kim was raised as a liberal Christian. Resilient, a planner, she has earned the equivalent of an MD and PhD in talking to doctors about what is going on with her daughter. Both are music educators. They teach children to love the beauty of music. They hear and almost seem to see the unseen.

And this is what I have seen in them. In this whole ordeal, they have learned to attend to the invisible: to the relational, to what really matters most—deep-down things. To what endures: to relationships of trust; to their love for one another (as different as they are in temperament and outlook); and to love for their older daughter, Abby, who is brilliant and creative but sometimes understandably feels left out. To their enduring gratitude to have doctors, whom they now trust, and who trust them. To have family, friends, and a religious community that supports them unconditionally. To beauty.

Where is God in all that they must face? It changes. At times it must feel like a fragile, invisible web that has to be tended. But there is something solid, if changing, underneath it all. Despite every change, every chance of loss, to be upheld by a reliable foundation to shared living. This is to know God. Not the static God of classical theism. That God is dead. But a God who sustains shared hope, as we reconstruct the connections, beyond every human loss and challenge.

PART FIVE

The Welcoming Rooms

CHAPTER NINE

A Home for Love

Rebecca Parker

You don't understand. If I were to agree with you, my whole faith would fall apart," my colleague, whom I'll call Sam, sputtered. He was clearly upset—physically shaking and red in the face. Both of us were seminary professors on the United Methodist study committee charged with reviewing the church's teachings on homosexuality. The church's position was proving to be highly divisive. On the one hand, the United Methodist Church taught that lesbians and gays were people of sacred worth whose civil rights needed protection. At the same time, it said that the practice of same-sex love was incompatible with Christian teaching. Ministers who were lesbian, gay, or bisexual were expected to be celibate or at least to keep their intimate relationships hidden. Same-sex couples could not count on their United Methodist congregations to bless and support their unions, welcome their children, or offer them pastoral care in times of illness or grief. Other mainline Christian denominations were similar.

Sam's outburst came because I'd suggested to him that

God's love, as revealed in the life and ministry of Jesus, called the church to affirm same-sex relationships. "From my perspective," I said to Sam, "God's love is experienced in unexpected surprises of grace and new insight. It stretches me and my community beyond our established norms into adventures in inclusiveness, greater solidarity with those we exclude as Other—including the Other within ourselves. To be a Christian is to be open to change, to move in the direction of deeper caring, compassion and courage. This is why our congregation voted to become a Reconciling Congregation—a congregation that publicly welcomes and affirms lesbian, gay, bisexual, and transgender people. This is our way of being faithful to Jesus."

My religious viewpoint threatened Sam to the core. As I listened to him voice his objections, I realized that he and I experienced love differently. Sam summarized his theology succinctly for me. He felt loved by God when he was obedient to God's rule. In his view, God's love was embodied in the "orders of creation"—the way God established the world at Creation as narrated in Genesis 1–3. In Sam's interpretation of these passages, God created humanity in two genders, male and female, and created woman to be man's helpmate. Patriarchal heterosexual union is the way God has ordained things to be. To deviate from it would be to turn away from God's love. Only by complying with the orders of creation could people receive God's love and be in right relationship with God. Furthermore, Sam explained, those who turn away from God's love will suffer the torments of the damned, and those who accept it will be rewarded with eternal life. God's love, he said, includes rewards and punishments, because human beings are nothing more than selfish, willful children. We are motivated by what gratifies us, by what we want, not what God wants. God disciplines us to teach us the right way to live, the way that accords with divine will.

For Sam, love was inseparable from a hierarchical structure of command and obedience. "Trust and obey for there's no other way to be happy in Jesus than to trust and obey," as an old familiar hymn put it. Only by living within such a structure did Sam feel loved, protected, cared for—right with himself and with the sacred. To agree with me, Sam felt he would have to abandon his core experience of what it meant to live within the embrace of God's love. The converse was true for me. I couldn't agree with Sam unless I walked away from the best that I knew love to be: the gift of gracious, transforming, unexpected invitation into greater life through increased connection and engagement with others, especially with those that the dominating society deemed Other.

The debates in Christian denominations over same-sex love have been under way for more than thirty years. Bitter, divisive, and heartbreaking for many, these struggles continue today. Their intensity is matched in the secular political sphere by the current state by state struggles over the civil right of same-sex couples to marry. Why is so much at stake? The global Anglican Church is fraught with conflict, and the controversy is kept alive by such people as Texas oil moguls who are pouring money into the hands of African church leaders to lobby them to oppose making the church more gay-friendly. What interest could oil industrialists possibly have in keeping the global Anglican Church from affirming same-sex relationships?

Apparently, love, as I and many religious progressives understand it, is dangerous. We advocate for love that surprises, disrupts, and alters the status quo; that expresses itself in diverse ways; that comes in rainbow colors. Those who want to preserve the existing social and economic order invest in prohibiting such love.

What will it take to bridge such a divide? The twenty-five members of the United Methodist Study Committee on Homosexuality well represented the diversity in the denomination. Committee members worked together for four years. Some of us felt strongly that there was a solid biblical and theological basis for the church to affirm same-sex intimacy within the identical guidelines that it affirmed heterosexual intimacy. We regarded sexuality as a positive, life-giving aspect of our humanity. We understood that an appropriate sexual ethic for all people was based in mutual care, fidelity, equality of power, and freedom of choice. We wanted to see the church bless and support the loving relationships formed between same-sex couples. We wanted the church to be a home for *all* who devoted their heart to family, to caring for one another, to loving generously and faithfully. Others felt that the whole foundation of Christian faith would crumble if the church took such a stand.

Over the course of its study, the committee consulted with experts in a wide range of fields: from biblical studies and theology to ethics, social science, biology, psychology, and medicine. Our thorough study and respectful conversation, however, did not suffice to bridge the deep differences in the church. At the end of four years, we all knew more, and we still disagreed. The committee recommended that the denomination pass a resolution noting that Christians sincerely disagreed on the issue of same-sex love and that United Methodists should continue in conversation, prayer, and study and should refrain from making any one position *the* position of the church. Our recommendation was not adopted. While I am confident that change will come, so far the United Methodist Church and many other Christian denominations have not affirmed same-sex couples.

What the United Methodist committee couldn't reconcile with any amount of civil dialogue were the fundamental differences among its members regarding *what it means to be human, what it means to live in right relationship with the divine, and what it means to love and be loved.* These are the topics of theological anthropology. Theological anthropology shapes the structures of meaning we live by and determines what kind of home we build for our families and for our spiritual lives. Through the work of the study committee, I learned that people can hold sharply different views on theological anthropology and that their views can go to the depths of their souls, defining their core sense of identity.

On the topics of theological anthropology, liberal and progressive people of faith have a distinctive history and an important perspective for the future. Sam represented a classic conservative Christian position, precisely the one that liberal theology has critiqued. Liberals reject the view that human beings are, by nature, selfish sinners, unable to choose what is right, driven by their rebellion against God's rule and in bondage to their needs and desires. Instead, religious liberals have taught that human beings are created in the image of God and possess sacred gifts that they must learn to use for good. Among these are the "powers of the soul," as the nineteenth-century liberal William Ellery Channing called them. The capacity for sexual intimacy and pleasure is one of the good gifts of God, along with the capacities of reason, feeling, imagination, language, memory, creativity, conscience, and more. Human existence is to be respected and reverenced as reflecting a divine origin.

In the early nineteenth century, liberal Christians in New England countered the dismal view of human nature taught by the prevailing Calvinist preachers who regarded people as "totally depraved" sinners from birth. The liberal message emphasized instead that humanity's divine origin is never fully defaced or erased by human folly and sin. "Love and reverence for human nature" are, Channing claimed, "the very spirit of Christianity." Basing their affirmation on early Christian doctrine, liberals said Christ restored the divine image in humanity and did so by incarnating the goodness, beauty, and power of God in his teaching, healing, and his resistance to evil and injustice. "One man was true to what is in us all," Ralph Waldo Emerson said of Jesus. Those who imitate Christ—who follow his example as a teacher—incarnate divinity through acts of compassionate love. As with Jesus, their love disrupts established social norms regarding who is welcome at the table of human fellowship. Radical inclusiveness is the mark of Christian love, for all bear the image of God.

The nineteenth-century progressives understood that human dignity—human potential to manifest divinity in the flesh—was not automatic. It had to be cultivated and nurtured—you had to grow a soul. The liberal Congregationalist Horace Bushnell taught that no child should ever have to lose her original connection to the divine, but that this connection could be lost if it wasn't nurtured. The purpose of education, Channing insisted, was to "call forth and direct aright all the powers of the soul." The powers of the soul were the image of God within us, and they would atrophy without exercise, or could be suppressed by social systems that denied humanity the full exercise of its powers.

Progressive social reform movements were rooted in liberal theological anthropology. Inspired by these Christian views, Horace Mann advocated for free public education so all children could develop their divine nature. Elizabeth Peabody led a movement to establish kindergartens in which children's native goodness was to be respected and nurtured. Progressive Christians opposed slavery and worked for abolition because slavery forcibly suppressed and denied the capacity of human beings to unfold their God-given gifts. As Channing argued:

> What is the end and essence of life? It is to expand all our faculties and affections. It is to grow, to gain by exercise

new energy, new intellect, new love. It is to hope, to strive, to bring out what is within us....Slavery is thus at war with the true life of human nature.

So, too, liberal Christian women and their allies worked to overturn the exclusion of women from education, from the vote, and from entrance into the professions, laboring to assure that women could exercise their full God-given human powers. Belief in the inherent goodness and worth of human beings led to outcries against every form of oppression and suppression. Exploitation, prejudice, and abuse of human beings were crimes against God as well as humanity. And humanity's divine nature was its authorization for revolt against injustice.

Some notable liberals, Emerson among them, spoke of humanity's freedom in individual terms and urged people to have courage to go it alone. But many others upheld relationality as central to human existence. Individual freedom mattered because it was a component in just community and life-giving communion among human beings. Early-twentieth-century liberal theology emphasized the social character of human existence. Belief in "the brotherhood of man" (to use their term) affirmed that all people are members of one family of humanity. Obligations to love and care for one another are implicit in life, not add-ons. We are bound together in "an inescapable net of mutuality," as Martin Luther King Jr. would say in advocating for racial and economic justice. What injures one diminishes all. Today, these remain countercultural values in a dominant social order that frequently tells us we are alone and have to look out for number one.

Throughout the history of liberal theological anthropology there runs a clear theme: love is not a vertical relationship of obedient submission to a divine ruler. As the liberal theologian Walter Rauschenbusch wrote: "We love and serve God when we love and serve our fellows." The powers of the soul enable connection and interaction with others. To be human is to be embedded in the intricate web of life. To be alive is to receive the world through all the channels of the senses, all the sensitive modes of feeling that are ours, and to respond with our own contribution. We give to life our touch, our word, our action, our embrace, our guidance, our acceptance, our censure, our blessing. All living is in community and in connection with others. Love is what happens in the vibrant interchange among living beings and life forms. It is the experience of being drawn to one another, of interacting with each other to create happiness and joy, to labor to care for life's daily needs, to give refreshment to the soul. Love blesses the intersections among individual beings and the whole fabric of existence.

Love's heart is nourished by pleasure and joy. Eros has an important place in spirituality. The Hebrew Bible includes the Song of Songs, which is full of juicy delight in human lovemaking. An ancient Christian baptismal hymn speaks of God as a divine lover uncovering the inward being of the beloved, filling her with his love, intoxicating her with water from his fountain, and carrying her into his paradise garden, "where in is the wealth of the Lord's pleasure." Joy and satisfaction are sparked when human and divine meet. Islamic spiritual poetry, likewise, uses erotic language, as the popular poetry of Rūmī and Hāfez illustrates.

Eros is more than *acceptable* in liberal religious understanding. It is *revelatory* of humanity's deepest capacities to touch and be touched, to take joy, to be transported and to transport another, to create life. Eros can be exploited and misdirected. It can be domesticated into patterns of dominance and submission that disrupt equality. When mutual power and consent are absent, it becomes abusive and can deeply harm souls and bodies. But, at its best, sexual intimacy can reveal the powers of the soul—our ability to feel and be affected, our capacity for both vulnerability and power, to receive and to give. It can teach us that we have agency to act in the world and that we can be moved deeply by the presence and the actions of another. It can transport our hearts into spaces of openness, flexibility, tenderness. It can renew, refresh, and satisfy our love for life—not only our affection for a beloved, but our affection for the world. Same-sex affectional and sexual relationships do all this, just as heterosexual relationships can.

I once took my grandmother Ernst to a Saturday workshop on lesbian sexuality and spirituality, offered by the well-known feminist-liberationist theologian Carter Heyward. My grandmother had asked me what feminist theology was all about, so I proposed we go together to the workshop. The workshop engaged us in thinking about the positive power of same-sex intimacy to foster commitments to mutuality in human relationships and to active work for social justice. Heyward emphasized that sexuality and spirituality were not polar opposites. Rather, the erotic dimension of life was sacred and could enhance our spirituality with insight, joy, and strength.

As we headed for home, I asked my grandmother what she thought of feminist theology. "I was rather hoping for something new!" she responded. "What?" I exclaimed, surprised that my grandmother, a Methodist minister's wife, was not taken aback by the day's themes. "Well," she explained, "I can see that feminist theology is rather like Quakerism: it looks to the authority of our own inner light—our experience—as a basis for religion." I saw her point and agreed. "But," she continued, "Dr. Heyward just said what I've always believed: our sexuality is part of everything we do that is creative and life giving. It isn't just about sex. Eros is involved in all our experiences of delight, and play, and caring. It permeates a good life."

I was astonished at my grandmother's progressive and beautiful regard for human sexuality. "How did you arrive at this view?" I asked her. "Did you come to this through your own inner light? Your experience? Is this your own theory?" "No," she retorted, and gave me a look that suggested I was hopelessly uninformed. "I learned this in my college class on human sexuality, of course!"

I should have known. My grandmother was a liberal Christian, and when she attended a church-related college in the 1920s the curriculum reflected the progressive Christian values of her era. Positive regard for human sexuality and respect for human experience as reflecting the image of God were core to those progressive values. We still need these values now. And we need them not only because our sexual and affectional lives matter for our personal happiness and well-being, but because they matter for the issues before our society—especially the problems of poverty and ecological sustainability.

At the dawn of the twenty-first century, progressive religion faces a new challenge, and theological anthropology is at the center. Serious economic difficulties are arising for many people. Overheated global market capitalism has produced chaos and uncertainty, and old questions need to be addressed in new ways. Can market capitalism be regulated to decrease the widening gaps between the wealthy elite and the poor and offer a decent life to more people? How can the economic inequalities between men and women, whites and people of color, be redressed? And how can the economic system that controls so much of our lives be transformed to turn the tide on ecological damage that threatens all life?

Transformation of our economy requires renewed attention to how we understand what it is to be human, what it is to be right with God, and what it means to love and be loved. The view of human nature that market capitalism trades on is precisely the view of human nature that my colleague Sam held. He saw all humans as by nature "depraved"—self-serving pleasure seekers desirous of life without any limits and unable to care for others or meet mature obligations. Theologian John Cobb observes that this is the dominant view of the human being in U.S. culture—the theological anthropology of the marketplace. *Homo economicus*—the economic human—of market capitalism is self-interested, focused on immediate gratification of wants and needs, and unconcerned with what happens to others in the process of getting his needs met. At every turn, the market—the dominant religion of our day—tells us and our children that this is who we are and who we should be. But this concept of the human being, in fact, diminishes and dehumanizes the fullness of who humans are and can be. And it tragically alienates human beings from the whole web of life on which all life depends.

How strange that the human depravity that Calvin saw and hoped would be redeemed by Christ has become the implicit view of human nature embedded in market capitalism. Economic practices based on regarding human beings as selfish and self-gratifying transfer wealth into the hands of an elite few. The marketplace *teaches* us to be self-interested and can make us captive to goals and values that don't help our communities and relationships to thrive. In the process, human kinship depreciates in value as does this good and beautiful earth.

According to early liberal theology, the antidote for the sin of human selfishness is the cultivation of selflessness. Love, in this perspective, takes no more important form than self-abnegation, self-sacrifice, and a willingness to suffer—like Christ on the cross—to be *for* others. This version of liberal theology reiterates a problematic "economy of salvation." Christ gives his life so humanity won't have to pay the price of its sins. Christ's life is exchanged for humanity's, and through this exchange humanity is redeemed from the debt it owes to God for its sins.

Love understood as self-sacrifice can harm life. When love

is identified with self-sacrifice, people are counseled to accept abuse that they should resist. Self-sacrificing love sometimes labors hard to protect perpetrators of sin from their obligations and responsibilities, carrying their burdens for them, protecting them from paying the cost of their choices. Such self-sacrificing love is unfair labor, theologian Delores Williams points out in her book *Sisters in the Wilderness.* Surrogate service is familiar to her as an African American woman. She observes that too many black women's lives have been worn down by providing the household help to raise other women's children and prepare food for families other than their own. These social practices and the theological ideas underpinning them are aligned with images of God as a householder whose slaves or servants do all the work. Taking the place of another to relieve her of her burdens never offers release for the servant.

In her book *Of Divine Economy: Refinancing Redemption,* theologian Marion Grau critiques this old "economy of salvation." She rereads ancient Christian texts on God as the master of a divine household—the *oikomenous.* The Greek word *oikos* (house) is the root of the word "economy." Instead of the head of a typical ancient Greek household in which women and slaves remain unfree, the God of her reimagining is "a courageous, hopeful investor in unpredictabilities." She suggests that God opposes economic models that maintain an unjust status quo and instead offers gifts and makes investments that disrupt the staid order of things, acting in the mix of chaos and creativity so as to instigate more freedom, more life, and more love.

The challenge for people of faith now is to counter market capitalism's joyless, diminished view of humanity and its life-threatening effects on earth's ecologies. We can't continue to build our economic house on the foundation of human depravity. We need to creatively transform our economic system with a different theological anthropology at its heart—one that regards human beings as generous, capable, and connected with one another and the earth.

To aim for zest and joy, and to resist oppression, is how process theology understands the impulse at the heart of all things, including the nature of human existence. Each being is unique and transitory, and all beings are connected. Each of us is a work in process. There is no "I" who exists through all time as an unchanging true "self." There is no enduring "subject" who "has" experiences the way a Christmas tree has ornaments. And there is no "self" who exists apart from interconnectedness with everything else that exists, including all other humans alive now and those who lived before. This relational, interactive, and fluid understanding of what it is to be human means that intimacy and connection are givens. Any notion of human existence as radically individual, isolated, or separate denies the nature of reality. Such a notion may be true to psychological states—people may *feel* alone. It also may be true to cultural and social conditionings—people may be taught to function *as if* they are self-interested individuals and that this is human nature. But what is truly natural—what is given in the nature of things—is interdependence. Because we are all connected, oppression, exploitation, and abuse touch everyone, not just some. Right relationship matters for all. None of us, in truth, exists in solitude. We all have belly buttons, as a colleague of mine was fond of pointing out. We are born from the bodies of others. We cannot exist without breathing and eating. Nor do we exist for ourselves alone. At the very least, we are interested in the future of our own self. Our own future self is an other for whom we must exercise care, as Charles Hartshorne explained in his essay "Beyond Enlightened Self-Interest." If we do not care for this other, life will not go on. And our own future self cannot be excised from the intricate web of life. Caring for multiple others—for all of life, ultimately—is integral to existence.

As we face the future, we need a rebirth of love for life, for the planet and for one another, grounded in a relational understanding of human existence. Love is more than obedience to divine authority or submission to the needs of others. It is not sufficiently expressed in powerless identification with those who suffer or paternalistic care of the pitied by the privileged. There needs to be a home for a different kind of love, one that celebrates erotic intimacy and happiness, that fosters play and pleasure among human beings, and that respects all people as created in the image of God and as possessing divine gifts of freedom and grace that enable us to love one another. There needs to be a home built on the understanding that all life is interdependent, whose foundation is faithful care, whose threshold is open-hearted welcome, whose kitchen serves any in need, and where love can lie down in peace and take joy. This kind of love can provide us the nourishment we need to resist the excesses and injustices of market capitalism. It can instigate more justice and sustainability for the planet.

If we can create a home for such love, it will indeed be a habitation that will offer hope for our world. At the threshold to such a home, the words of Rūmī could justly be inscribed:

You that love Lovers,
This is your home. Welcome!

(translated by Coleman Barks)

CHAPTER TEN

The Welcome Table

John Buehrens

The sign said, "Everyone Welcome." But this was the segregated South, sixty years ago. White folks were gathering
to form a new, progressive church in Knoxville: academics,
union leaders, professionals, activists, students. "Does that
mean me, too?" asked the black man. "It sure does!" said the
greeter. It wasn't a very large congregation. But Jim Pearson
became a member. Soon the music director was another black
man, Calvin Dash. Leaders of the Knoxville black community
joined, and a multiracial congregation was born. They helped
to form an area Council on Human Relations that began to offer summer camps where black and white children could simply
play together and get to know one another. Church members
volunteered. Often they had to move the camp's site because
the Ku Klux Klan put bombs in mailboxes or left threats. After
the Supreme Court ruling in 1954, the church voted to take out
a full-page ad in the local newspaper, urging citizens to support
implementing school desegregation "with all deliberate speed."
Many of the local sit-ins to desegregate public facilities were

organized at the church. When Martin Luther King Jr. was killed before the Poor People's March on Washington could happen, the church organized meals for the protesters.

The congregation did not stop at issues of race. I served as their minister in the 1970s. When Knoxville gay and lesbian Christians formed a small Metropolitan Community Church, no one would provide them with worship space. So we did. They met Sunday afternoons. Then early one Sunday evening the front windows of the church building were shot out by young men in a pickup truck. They threw formaldehyde into the building. Our youth group was meeting in another room. We cleaned up, called the police, and calmed fears. But we didn't call the media. Few people would have been sympathetic. We just focused on staying open and hospitable.

All this came back to me in August 2008. A man entered the sanctuary of my former congregation on a summer Sunday with a shotgun hidden in his guitar case. The diverse children of this welcoming congregation had been working on a musical together, *Annie Junior.* That Sunday morning they were present-ing it.

He left a four-page letter in his vehicle saying that he was frustrated at not being able to get a job and that he blamed all the problems in his life and in the world on "liberals." A truck driver with multiple drunken-driving convictions, he had been married and divorced five times. His fifth wife had taken out a restraining order on him before she divorced him. For a time, before she chose to leave Knoxville, she had attended this church, where the concerns of abused women are taken seriously. His goal, his note said, was to kill as many liberals as possible before police killed him. He had lots of shells. His apartment was full of right-wing literature blaming everything on liberals—books by Sean Hannity, Bill O'Reilly, and Mi-chael Savage.

When he came in, aiming his shotgun at a chancel full of children, the head usher, Greg McKendry, stepped into the line of fire. He took the shotgun blast to his own chest. The next shots killed a visitor, Linda Kraeger, and wounded six other adults. John Bohstedt, a history professor who was to play "Daddy Warbucks" in the children's musical, joined another church member in wrestling the shooter to the ground. A week later, the minister, Chris Buice, commented, "He believed that liberals were soft on terror. He had a rude discovery!" They held him down until police and paramedics arrived. Meanwhile, the children were taken to safety at the Presbyterian church next door, where, the following evening, more than a thousand people gathered in solidarity with the hated so-called liberals.

I was there the next Sunday for the rededication of the sanctuary. A reporter asked Buice what he wanted from a day in court. "Justice," he said. "What would justice look like?" "A community where our children are safe," he replied. The man pleaded guilty as charged, saying it was "the honorable thing to do." He was sentenced to life in prison, no parole. His victims and their loved ones accept that. They have little interest in state-sponsored murder as revenge. As Dr. King said, "An eye for an eye and a tooth for a tooth and soon we shall all be eyeless and toothless."

The outpouring of love the Knoxville church received from neighbors of all faiths and convictions has helped the healing. Their conviction that love is stronger than death and more powerful than hate is not weakened, but deepened. So the sign is still there. "Everyone Welcome." And the church really means it: anyone who comes in peace is welcome.

That church is not alone. In countless places, progressive churches have welcomed new groups getting started to meet some unmet moral or spiritual need in the community: women's groups, environmental groups, recovery groups. At the core of authentic religion is the spirit of hospitality. All three Abrahamic faiths recognize this. The tent of Abraham is open on all four sides to welcome the stranger from anywhere, say the rabbis. The infamous sin of ancient Sodom was not same-sex love, scholars say, but rather a brutal violation of strangers who should have been treated with hospitality.

There is much to forgive in this world. Those who have been hurt often know that best. But hospitality, rightly practiced, can be a powerful source of healing. Patrick Thomas Aquinas O'Neill (I love that name!), now minister of the First Unitarian Church in Brooklyn, tells this story from his own childhood: He was in first grade. One day that winter, some older boys pushed him, face first, into a snowbank. Outraged at the indignity, he sat crying on the front stoop of his house. A neighbor, Mrs. Boutellon, had seen everything. She came out, brushed the snow off his clothes, and took him to her kitchen table. She served him hot cocoa and told him, in her French accent, "Patrick, you are angry at those boys for what they did to you. And it is natural for you to feel that way. But now—you must let it go. This day has other things to give you."

Patrick never forgot what she said. Years later, after both Mrs. Boutellon and her husband had died, he told his mother about it. "That sounds just like her," said Mrs. O'Neill. "You know, don't you, that the Boutellons were both survivors of the Nazi concentration camps?"

In the Sermon on the Mount, Jesus tells his followers to seek forgiveness and be reconciled to one another before they bring their gifts to the altar of God. This is a rigorous standard, but spiritually sound. Conrad Browne, who with his wife, Ora, and their children lived as part of the interracial Christian community called Koinonia, in southern Georgia in the early '50s, says that it was a part of daily practice there. Before evening prayers, members were encouraged to ask forgiveness of anyone with whom they had tension during the day. It helped, especially when under pressure from the Klan and a boycott. "Be angry but do not sin," it says in the fourth chapter of the Epistle to the Ephesians. "Do not let the sun go down on your anger."

"Forgive us our trespasses as we forgive others who trespass against us," says the prayer Jesus taught. Some Christian theologies emphasize the experience of forgiveness *through* Jesus. Other, more radical and progressive theologies emphasize the subsequent challenge of also laying down any right to revenge. When a gunman entered a one-room Amish schoolhouse a few years ago and killed five young girls before killing himself, the response of Amish parents astonished many people. They attended the man's funeral and even prayed for him. Their way of life may be quite different, but many progressive theologians understood. It is not the point of the Gospels to feel forgiven and then be free to hate or judge.

"We are in the early stages of a radical reassessment of Jesus," writes progressive evangelical author Brian D. McLaren. Like many in more traditional mainline churches, he represents a growing number of Christians, including younger evangelicals and those in the "emerging church" movement, who are asking new questions. What, for example, should it mean for their faith today that Jesus so clearly juxtaposed his own radical hospitality with the conventional religiosity of his own time? Or that when Jesus preached about the kingdom of God as a discipleship of equals, he was so clearly challenging the domination system embodied in the pretensions of Rome to global imperial hegemony—pretensions that America seems to have in our own time?

"Why do we need to have singular and firm opinions on the protection of the unborn, but not about how to help poor people and how to avoid killing people labeled enemies who are already born?" McLaren asks. "Or why are we so concerned about the legitimacy of homosexual marriage but not about the legitimacy of fossil fuels or the proliferation of weapons of mass destruction (and in particular, *our weapons* as opposed to *theirs*)? Or why are so many [evangelicals] arguing about the origin of species but so few concerned about the extinction of species?"

McLaren understands Jesus's message in the way progressive theology often has: not as being about "escaping this troubled world for heaven's blissful shores, as is popularly assumed, but instead as about God's will being done on this troubled earth as it is in heaven." It is about having the faith that we can together feed the many who are hungry—because, just as Jesus is said to have fed five thousand with two fishes and a few loaves of bread, with plenty left over, we need to operate out of an awareness of abundance, not a model of scarcity. Jesus spread a welcome table for all people, and we are called to do the same.

We have for too long turned the market into our modern god. But it is an impotent idol when it comes to creating authentic justice and peace. The judgments of the unfettered market, as the recent global economic crisis has amply demonstrated, are *not*, as Psalm 19 describes God's judgments, "true and righteous altogether." That is mere free market fundamentalism. We forget that when markets emerged in human history, bringing peoples of different customs and laws together, the more universalizing forms of religion emerged to urge the powerful to remember to treat others as they themselves would want to be treated.

We are now in a time when even the prosperous among us are facing reduced expectations and economic anxieties. It may be a good time to face another challenging question that isn't asked often enough: "How much do I (or we) deserve, anyway?" Recently I was asked to address a congregation exploring concerns about global hunger. The congregation had decided to raise money and consciousnesses simultaneously by holding a "hunger banquet." Perhaps you have been to one. Since we live in a world of more than six billion people, where at least two billion live on the equivalent of $2 a day or less, a third of those present were served only small portions of plain rice. Others received rice and beans and a vegetable. Only about one out of ten people were served what most of us would call "a full meal," including dessert. And only a few people out of a hundred got a "gourmet meal" that evening.

As I told the gathering, I had recently done some Christmas shopping at a glitzy mall nearby. I was laden down with my own purchases, tired, contemplating the competitive aspects of our culture's great annual consumer potlatch, muttering to myself ("This is how we celebrate the birth of Christ in a stable?"), and pondering how even gift-giving now gets tainted with sneaky forms of competition and ego gratification. Just then I caught sight of a teenage boy, just bobbing along, listening to his iPod, nothing in hand, wearing a T-shirt with a memorable slogan: "Only YOU can prevent narcissism!" How refreshing, I thought, to see the key spiritual ailment of our culture named there in its very temple! Its message is embedded in every ad we hear or see: "What matters is *you; what you feel,* what you *want,* and, above all, *what you deserve.*"

On the way home, I popped into the CD player in my car a gift that I had bought (from me to me, with love): a recording of those amazing women who call themselves Sweet Honey In The Rock. They were singing a Bernice Johnson Reagon song about how to talk about greed. "Greed is so sneaky," they sang. "Hard to detect in myself; I see it so clearly in everybody else." Immediately I thought of the passage in Matthew in which a rich young man asks Jesus what he must do to have life eternal. Jesus first asks, "Why do you call me good? There is only One who is good." Then he tells him to keep the commandments. "Which ones?" Jesus says don't murder, commit adultery, steal, or bear false witness. Honor your father and mother. Love your neighbor as yourself. "But I do; what then do I still lack?" "Jesus said, 'If you wish to be perfect, go, sell all you have, give the money to the poor, and you will have treasure in heaven, then come, follow me.' When the young man heard this, he went away sorrowful, for he had many possessions."

Like him, most of us don't feel called to be perfect. But how can we denounce every public effort to help the poor and vulnerable of our society as an "entitlement" while simultaneously maintaining a culture that seems shot through with entitlement? The great sociologist Robert Bellah once observed that "it is no accident that...the United States, with its high valuation of the individual, is nonetheless the only North Atlantic society where such a high percentage of people live in poverty. Just when we are moving into an ever-greater valuation of the sacredness of the individual person, our capacity to imagine a social fabric that would hold individuals together is vanishing. And this is in no small part due to the fact that our religious individualism is linked to an economic individualism which, though it makes no distinction between persons except monetary ones, ultimately know nothing of sacredness. For if the only standard is money, then all other values are undermined."

In the Gospel of Matthew, when the rich young man goes away, Jesus remarks that it will be as hard for a camel to pass through the eye of a needle as for a person laden with riches to enter into the spiritual commonwealth ruled by God. "Then how can anyone be saved?" ask his disciples. With God's openness, all things are possible, Jesus replies. Then he tells a parable.

The owner of a vineyard goes out in the morning to hire laborers. He agrees to give them the usual daily wage. Seeing more people seeking work, and more to be done, he goes out later and tells those people he will pay them what is right as well. He does the same at noon, midafternoon, and just an hour before quitting time at sunset. When payment time comes, he orders that the last hired be the first to be paid, and that they receive a full day's wage. Those who worked all day grumble out loud. But the owner of the vineyard replies, "Am I allowed to do what I choose with what is mine? Or are you envious because I am generous?"

So how much *do* we deserve? In a book with that title, Richard Gilbert suggests some religious principles for distributive justice. Among other things, Gilbert quotes what the U.S. Catholic bishops wrote in a pastoral letter in 1986:

> Distributive justice…calls for the establishment of a floor of material well-being on which all can stand. This is the duty of the whole of society, and it creates particular obligations for those with greater resources. This duty calls into question extreme inequalities of income and consumption when so many lack basic necessities. Catholic social teaching does not maintain that a flat, arithmetic equality of income and wealth is a demand of justice, but it does challenge economic arrangements that leave large numbers of people impoverished. Further, it sees extreme inequality as a threat to the solidarity of the human community, for great disparities lead to deep social divisions and conflicts.

When my congregation contemplates efforts to help the poor, whether through charity or through improved social arrangements, there are always those who wonder whether the help is going to the "deserving" poor. I have only one basic theological response to that. It's a matter of sisterhood and brotherhood, of spiritual equality around the table that God has set before us. So when we are troubled by what some call the "internalized oppression" of the victimized and see self-defeating patterns of behavior in the poor, we might try maintaining empathy and solidarity the way psychologist Mary Pipher says a good marriage is kept together: try looking in the mirror and then saying, "You know, you're no prize either!"

Because there is no one around God's welcome table who is entirely free of some self-defeating flaw. No, not one. Yet only you, and you, and you, and you and I together can even begin to prevent narcissism. Or prevent a culture of narcissistic self-involvement and entitlement from sapping empathy and generosity from our very souls. Only then can we begin to talk around the table about greed—and learn to pass the potatoes more politely. And to discuss not an ideology, but a spirituality and theology that moves toward a welcome table of abundance for all God's children. One aimed at reducing the violence and anger in the world by living more simply, so that others may simply live, by practicing responsible consumption, and by supporting something closer to a living wage (not a minimum wage) for more of our sisters and brothers.

Every spring my family gathers to celebrate Passover, the festival of liberation, around my sister-in-law's table. As a progressive Jew, she calls us to a "freedom seder": one focused on the hope that next year *all* God's children shall dwell in the city of peace, where *shalom* is created by having a community in which all children are safe and have enough to eat. And often when I receive or celebrate Christian Communion, I do so in the same spirit. It is a spirit of hoping that I have laid down enough bitterness and anger to be able to go away humming in my heart that old song that says, "We're gonna sit at the welcome table, one of these days." Of knowing that I have been welcomed already—and blessed, and spiritually fed, and sent forth to try to make it possible for more people in this world to see that we don't really *deserve* anything. Everything we receive in this life is a gift; a gift to be shared around the welcome table with our hungry sisters and brothers.

CHAPTER ELEVEN

A Sanctuary for the Spirit

John Buehrens and Rebecca Parker

T he people of Le Chambon, a small village in France, har-bored hundreds of Jewish children during World War II. Years later, when they were visited by one of the children— now a grown man—who had been sheltered there, he found himself asking why that village had sheltered Jewish children when so many others had not. He found his answer in observing their simple worship practices. Le Chambon was a Huguenot, Protestant village. A religious minority, accustomed to struggling to survive, they regularly gathered to sing hymns, to recall the faith of ancestors who had held fast to the spirit of love even in times of trial, to offer thanksgiving, and to pray for one another. When he asked them to explain, they said that they could not imagine responding in any other way. It was simply the shape that their souls had. Their ways of worship had formed them for courage and resistance.

"Sanctuary," Elie Wiesel says, "is often something very small. Not a grandiose gesture, but a small gesture toward alleviating human suffering and preventing humiliation. Sanctuary is a human being. Sanctuary is a dream. That is why you are here and that is why I am here; we are here because of one another. We are in truth each other's shelter."

"Will you harbor me, will I harbor you?" asks Ysaye Barnwell in one of the songs she wrote and sings with Sweet Honey In The Rock. Singing and praying together and telling stories of faith and courage can shape us to be faithful to the Spirit. Through such ritual we can be formed to more fully embody what the world most needs.

Today, many people say, "I am spiritual but not religious." They want to connect more deeply with the Spirit, but they have little confidence that the Spirit is going to show up at a worship service or religious ritual. They may be right. Even in the Bible, the Spirit shows up on mountaintops, along roadsides, and in humble homes and rooms more often than it does in designated places of worship, ritual, and assembly. Both biblical languages use the same word for spirit and for the wind. "The *pneuma* (spirit) blows where it chooses," says the Gospel of John. But if we are going to more fully realize the commonwealth of God, we need a *pneumatology* that goes beyond the highly individualistic, narcissistic "spirituality" of contemporary culture. We need one that helps to identify how we can cultivate collective responsiveness to the Spirit that truly makes for holiness and wholeness. Human beings often need sanctuary. But so does the Spirit.

At one of the first worship services we led together, John preached, and Rebecca played the cello. The sermon was about an incident that took place in Sarajevo, Bosnia, in 1992. The principal cellist of the Sarajevo Opera, Vedran Smailovic, heard a mortar shell burst in the street near his home, quickly followed by screams. People had been standing in line to buy bread from one of the few remaining bakeries in the violence-ravaged city. When he looked out his window, Vedran saw the carnage. The shell killed twenty-two people. Grieved and shocked, he felt he must do something. But what? He did what he felt he, as an artist, could do. Dressed up in his formal concert clothes, he went out the next afternoon and sat where the shell had burst and played the plaintive Albinoni *Adagio in G Minor.* He played every afternoon for the next twenty-two days, one day of music for every person killed. Then he kept playing, day after day. As Swati Chopra describes his discipline and his music:

> He played to ruined homes, smouldering fires, scared peo-
> ple hiding in basements. He played for human dignity that
> is the first casualty in war. Ultimately, he played for life,
> for peace, for the possibility of hope that exists even in
> the darkest hour. Asked by a journalist whether he was not
> crazy doing what he was doing, Smailovic replied: "You ask
> me if I am crazy for playing the cello. Why do you not ask
> if they are not crazy for shelling Sarajevo?"

As Rebecca played the Albinoni *Adagio,* John asked those at worship to open themselves to the same Spirit that had guided this highly courageous act of solidarity and resistance. A few rare individuals may have an innate instinct for courage. But most of us gain the spiritual strength to stand by one another, beyond the boundaries of difference or in the midst of tragic injustice, only by learning to do so. It takes practice, just as playing music does.

Psychologist Eva Fogelman, in her book *Conscience and Cour-age,* asks why some Gentiles risked their lives to give sanctuary to Jews during the Holocaust, but she does not find a definitive answer. She finds no common psychological profile or shared pattern of belief or disbelief. She ends her inquiry with a more contemporary story:

A woman named Hannah was walking through a market-place in Jerusalem. Suddenly this forty-year-old mother of eight heard someone shouting, "Terrorist! Arab!" A young man ran past her and was tackled by a soldier right at her feet. Adnan al-Afandi, age twenty-one, a young Muslim extremist, had stabbed a thirteen-year-old Jewish boy. The crowd closed in. Hannah felt something terrible was about to happen. Someone fired a shot. Without thinking, she threw herself atop the young Arab to protect him. The crowd was shocked. They spit on her, kicked her, cursed her, and called her "Arab lover! Traitor!" and worse. Hannah stayed put until the police took al-Afandi into custody. In the weeks that followed, her actions were fiercely debated in Israel. She came from a community of *haredim,* Jews called "ultra-orthodox." She further violated stereotypes about them, and about women among them, by agreeing to go on television with the mother of the boy who had been stabbed. On television, the mother screamed, "I am very angry at this woman, more than at the terrorist!" and said that she would have preferred that the crowd had killed al-Afandi right there in the market. Hannah just replied, "I gave him sanctuary as a human being—as a child of God—and now I must explain myself?"

Religion is often divisive. But what if this is only *empty* religion—religion that emphasizes more the defensive shell of identity than the authentic Spirit it is meant to contain and shelter? Mind you, some people who have given up on religion and on worship may have more of this authentic Spirit in them than sixty pious people sitting in pews or otherwise worshipping together. But what if the real solution to religious strife is not to empty out the houses of worship but to fill them up again, with the Spirit?

John often calls himself "a Unitarian of the Third Person"—referring to the classic doctrine of "three persons" in the Trinity: Father, Son, and Holy Spirit. John identifies the Spirit behind the Creation and in all the prophetic witnesses to the redemption of history from injustice and violence and in Jesus with the one Spirit that faith says still proceeds from these (and other) sources. It is Holy because it yearns for harmony, justice, wholeness. Like a sanctuary, it has at least three dimensions. In planning, leading, or teaching worship, he emphasizes all three: height, depth, and breadth.

Some people today seem to want worship to be only one-dimensional: "uplifting." They compartmentalize the Spirit to a vertical realm to avoid mixing their spirituality with horizontal matters, with the ethical outrages that show up every day in the world. For them, these belong to other compartments—politics, economics, sports, or entertainment. They want worship leaders who may touch on the latter two realms—preferably with lightness and humor—but *never* on the more serious issues of human relations that are economic or political. And in a consumer culture, where religion itself becomes a commodity, such preachers are reliably popular. Again: "There is nothing quite so saleable in religion," said James Luther Adams, "than egoism wrapped in idealism."

Surely authentic openness to the Spirit does have a vertical dimension, and not just in shared worship. "Religion," said Whitehead, "is what a man does with his solitude." Many people treasure moments of solitude in which they are able to feel and remember how good the gift of life is. Such moments can be as ordinary as stepping into the shower in the morning and finding oneself drenched in gratitude—for clean, hot water; for just being alive, for the grace-filled opportunity to wash away mistakes of the past and to begin a new day afresh. But in the psalms, which have guided generations in learning the dynamics of the Spirit, there is something more multidimensional than "uplifting." A given psalm, like the whole collection, may end with praise. But along the way there will also be honest meditation on times of deep despair and feelings of abandonment, betrayal, and envy of those who seem to prosper without caring either for God or their fellow humans.

Just as the horizontal plane of religion is about the ethical question of justice, so the horizontal plane of worship is about the breadth or inclusiveness of its welcome. More inclusive language, greater lay participation in testimony and in "the prayers of the people," broader musical diversity—all these can stretch congregations to make more ample room for one another and for the Spirit. A great liberal liturgist once said that in worship we should do two things: first, "let the horizon of our minds include all people, the great family here on earth with us now," and then include "those who have gone before and left to us the heritage of their memory and their work; and those whose lives will be shaped by what we do or leave undone." Too much worship, even among liberals, does only the first part. Priding itself on being contemporary and inclusive, it easily substitutes a seemingly chummy, but secretly clubby, kind of informality for any true sense of awe before the "great cloud of witnesses" who have gone before and the prayerful aspiration they might summon us to. This constitutes insufficient room for the fullness of the Spirit. Too many worshipping communities have also blocked the Spirit by getting caught up in "worship wars"—worrying and arguing more about ancestral stylistics than about the spiritual substance at the heart of good worship.

Good worship is the shared work of the people gathered. In the Puritan plainness of the Needham meetinghouse, with its clear glass windows and lack of adornment, the earliest records of common worship authorized one of the deacons, back in the early 1700s, to "tune the psalm"—that is, to lead the singing. All worship, no matter how simple, is a form of "liturgy"— from the Greek words *leitos* (people) and *ourgia* (work)—the people's spiritual work, to get back in touch with the Spirit, in its varied dimensions, and in its transforming wholeness. Even

Quakers have a liturgy—of waiting, in silence, until someone feels prompted by the Spirit to speak. Many other Protestants do not realize how deeply their basic pattern of worship comes from ancient synagogue practice: a prayer of invocation; a psalm chanted (or later a hymn sung, many growing out of psalms); a scriptural reading or two; prayers; a sermon explicating and applying the spiritual wisdom of the scriptures; a final psalm or hymn; and a blessing. In many Christian groups, this constitutes "the liturgy of the Word," often then followed by the "liturgy of the Table," or Eucharist, from the Greek verb for giving thanks.

For worship to be "in spirit and in truth," it should have a dimension of depth as well as breadth and height—with time for confession, for honest meditation on the depths to which we human beings can sink, for acknowledging the tragic dimensions of life, and for intercession—praying that the brokenness and hurts within and among us be healed.

Preaching can and often should encompass these dimensions as well. In times of public crisis, like our own, it is important for wise worship leaders not to tell people *what* to feel, but to design worship that embraces the full range of human emotions present, and then allows the Spirit to channel them back toward basic gratitude, love, and courage. Certainly the more the sermon deals with public issues, the more important it is for the preacher to remember that somewhere in the sanctuary there is someone saying to him- or herself, "I'm giving the Spirit just one more chance today to tell me why I should go on."

No wonder fear and trembling accompany worship leaders honest about the task! They aren't in the chancel or pulpit or on the *bima* to please the people before them. Instead, their accountability is less to those who sit in front them and more to what stands behind them, sensing that if they were to turn around and try to see the Spirit face to face, they might be struck dead for not living up to the challenge of prophetic courage. Though the depths are not to be dodged, worshippers are there to be tugged forward in hope. One great liberal minister we both knew ended every service with an allusion to the mission that Jesus called his own—"that we might have life, and life more abundant"—before sending his people out to love and serve others to help fulfill that end.

The path to more abundant life needs a sustaining spirit of gratitude and praise. Liberal worship sometimes suffers from an underlying anger and disappointment at the state of the world, as if mere outrage were in and of itself a source of healing and empowerment. It is not. "A person will worship something," said Emerson. "Have no doubt about that. We may think that our tribute is paid in secret in the dark recesses of our hearts—but it will out. That which dominates our imaginations and thoughts will determine our lives, and character. Therefore it behooves us to be careful about what we worship, for what we are worshipping we are becoming."

The late Donald Barthelme once wrote a short story called "On Angels" that can be read as a parable set in heaven of the need for right worship here on earth. The story imagines the crisis that took place in heaven after the death of God. Up to that point the angels had been primarily occupied in singing praises to the Eternal—when not on errands delivering messages of warning, comfort, or blessing. (The word *angelos* in Greek means "messenger.") The core of the story is an interview on television with one of the chief angels about how they are coping now that God is finally gone. After God's death, the angel replies, they tried worshipping Nature—stars, planets, moons, and so on. Soon each of them was pointed in a different direction, however. There was no longer any real coherence to their worship or to their community. So for a time they tried worshipping one another. When that proved disappointing, various angels proposed various messages, ideals, slogans, and mottos. But soon they were just competing, arguing over which to worship. "We are still searching for a new principle," the angel ends by saying.

As God knows, many old, outworn images of God *have* now died. Thank God! But too much of what today is called "spirituality" seems more like what a friend calls "bottled fog." It lacks the full dimensions of a progressive and engaged faith that can shelter the Spirit of Life in all of its depth, breadth, and height. Perhaps this is why music remains so central to sustaining the human spirit: because it alone can express the full range and tempo of our spiritual lives. Like the Spirit itself, music seems able to "help us in our weakness," as Paul phrases it in Romans 8. "For we do not know how to pray as we ought, but the very Spirit intercedes with sighs too deep for words." The spirituality of an engaged and prophetic faith, whether it is being practiced in the rehearsal hall known as a "sanctuary," or out in the streets in protests, or through online organizing, petitions, or stockholder activism, is always in protection of human dignity, and is always going to require music for sustenance. Every activist knows that.

After all, there is a music already sounding before we even enter this life. As Adrienne Rich says in her poem, "Transcendental Etude," it seems that "before we've even begun to read or mark time, we're forced to begin in the midst of the hardest movement, the one already sounding as we are born." The world's harsh and sweet music has been clattering, humming, and pounding for a long time. The "buzzing, blooming confusion," the cacophony surrounding our lives, includes harsh realities, legacies of injustice, war, violence, and dehumanization. It is almost impossible to live in the contemporary world without feeling bombarded by noise and images that intrude like spam on every moment. Some may try to respond with new forms of asceticism—turning off the television, the computer, and seeking more silence. But such a sterile iconoclasm is ultimately powerless before the great flow of sounds and images. Instead, we need communal worship and personal spiritual practice that can teach us to hear and make a counterpoint music. As song-writer Carolyn McDade makes clear, we need music that tunes our souls to give "life the shape of justice."

Worship and spiritual practices at best give artful shape to the capacities of the human soul—its capacity to give sanctuary to both the animating Spirit and to other lives. All our living, from earliest childhood, is a process of experiencing, interpreting, and acting in the world. And we humans are communal from beginning to end—interactive, social, embedded in culture and history. Religion, most comprehensively defined, is about re-presenting the world to us in an interpretive way that will enhance human living. No wonder there is no human culture without art and ritual to teach souls how to sing and feel and hold hope amid all the cacophony that we are born into.

The ancient philosophers of Greece understood the power of the arts to reshape human experience better than some moderns do. In talking about music in relationship to education, Aristotle argues that it "has the power of forming the character....There seems to be in us a sort of affinity to musical modes and rhythms, which make some philosophers say that *the soul is a tuning.*" He describes the effect that music can have in terms that every leader, whether of worship or of a protest rally, might do well to bear in mind. Music is multidimensional. It can lighten or delight the soul; it can arouse passion for action; it can evoke feelings of pity, fear, or compassion. For Aristotle, art and music are never ethically neutral. They can stir up passion for violence and war; they can also be used to heal or transform. Some sacred melodies, he writes, "excite the soul to mystic frenzy," leaving people "restored as though they had found healing and purgation."

The late-fourth-century African theologian, Augustine, wrote a treatise on music, building on these philosophical traditions. "The soul performs a variety of temporal rhythms," he says in *De Musica*. The different states of the soul—equanimity, unrest, desire, reverie—accord with music's differing rhythmic patterns. If the music pulses with true joy, the kind that does not ignore despair, it can move a soul from great melancholy to praise, even from death to life. In some early Christian visual art, Christ is even portrayed using the iconography of the Greek god-man Orpheus, the god of music. Recall that Orpheus lost his love in the underworld. He journeyed there to rescue her, making it past the gates of hell by charming its fierce guards with his sweet music.

The spirituals and sorrow songs of the African American experience witness to the power of song and poetry to save life when it is most at risk. Theologian Howard Thurman wrote of this music and its role in resistance to and escape from oppression, saying in his autobiography,

> There can be…no opening of the heart to the flow of the living spirit of the living God, no raw laceration of the nervous system created by the agony of human suffering, pain, or tragedy; there can be no thing that does not have within it the signature of God, the Creator of Life, the living substance out of which all particular manifestations of life arise.…Always, against all that fragments and shatters and against all things that separate and divide within and without, life labors to meld together in a single harmony.

"Beauty will save us," says Dostoevsky's character Prince Myshkin in *The Idiot*. The arts, like good worship, can teach us to feel keenly the complex emotions that orient the soul to make greater room for the Spirit. They can also restore the soul when it is depleted, when it has become anesthetized, bored, satiated, shut down, or fragmented.

Despite all these affirmations about the significance of the arts as a shelter for the Spirit, the monotheistic faiths have often worried about the place of the arts within religion, sometimes seeing them as potentially idolatrous. Protestant reformers destroyed visual images, purged worship of any sensual rituals, and expelled musical instruments. For some iconoclasts, this expressed the idea that the flesh must be crucified and the senses and passions crushed rather than channeled. Others countered that such a move denied the very incarnation of the divine, the presence of the Spirit of God in the flesh. So German pietists of the seventeenth century quarreled over what constituted sacred music. Some wanted no music that would arouse any bodily feelings or emotions, they were opposed to music with strong rhythms or moving melodies that might evoke grief, outrage, or even joy. Others argued that music assisted the life of the soul precisely by its capacity to touch the full range of human emotions. Music for them was analogous to the Spirit's descent into flesh.

Johann Sebastian Bach, despite the disfavor of some in the church hierarchy, held the latter view: that music should animate the body and emotions just as the Spirit fills and transforms our earthly existence. His advocacy of emotion in music kept him from some of the most lucrative musical posts of his time. Notice that this argument between music that evokes emotions and music that lulls the listener into serene impassivity continues today. As if such ethereal "spirituality" could make one close to God or to one's fellow suffering creatures!

Progressive religion in the twenty-first century will be stronger if it can engage not only music but also the visual arts in developing a house for the Spirit, a house for hope. Many Americans today gather in megachurch sanctuaries that exude the aesthetics of shopping malls or sports arenas. The spaces are purged of anything too "churchy"—which surely has marketing advantages, given how alienated from "religion" many people today are. But this accommodation of American religion to the world of consumerism, aided and abetted by Protestant iconoclasm, lacks full power to reshape the imagination as a true home for the Spirit. Early Christians knew better. Their worship spaces were filled with beauty, giving a sense of paradise now to those whose eyes brought them there for the rituals of baptism, Eucharist, and shared worship.

"Everything belongs to the God of beauty," said the second-century Christian theologian Clement of Alexandria, and "everything subsists in the God of Beauty." Today's bland visual world in most churches does little either to veil or disclose the Holy. Sacred Eros has drained away. Music helps, but the disembodied Word, above all, is counted on to call and convert and stir. This is an anorexic diet, insufficient for a progressive faith that truly wants to inspire great love for life in this beautiful world. To give its faith greater form, progressive religion must learn to become practiced and disciplined in the creation, use, and interpretation of images, not just words and music.

After all, "the great surmise," as one of our friends puts it, that is both hidden and revealed in Creation's beauty, is that we creatures were and are loved—more than we can say or sing. Yet before we can truly begin to love others, much less practice the love that embodies itself as sanctuary and as justice, we must remember and reimagine that love. Images, symbols, and songs are the medium for such memory and imagination. They show us the way, and then they yield to the mystery they reveal. An

old hymn by the Quaker poet John Greenleaf Whittier puts it
this way:

> Blow, winds of God, awake and blow the mists of earth
>   away;
> Shine out, O Light Divine and show how wide and far we
>   stray.
> The letter fails, the systems fall, and every symbol wanes:
> The Spirit over-brooding all, Eternal Love, remains.

PART SIX

The Threshold

CHAPTER TWELVE

No Caravan of Despair

Rebecca Parker

E very theological house has its doorway—its point of entrance and departure. We now come, toward the end of this book, to the doors of our theological house. Thresholds are sacred places symbolizing the permeable boundary between a community's inner circle and the wider world. They mark the importance of movement between shelter and adventure—of arriving home and of setting out. They invite reflection on the relationship between those inside and those outside a given framework of meaning.

How do we regard the Other who is outside our theological house? And what does it mean to be one theological house in a world of many religions? These questions fall into the classic theological topic of "missiology"—mission and evangelism. One familiar Christian approach frames outsiders as nonbelievers who need to be saved. From this perspective there is only one true household of faith, and the mission of the religious community is to make all outsiders into insiders, to convert and assimilate the Other. Another perspective is possible. A theological house can be a place of hospitality to any who seek its shelter; it can honor religious diversity and welcome creative exchange among multiple religious practices and perspectives. It can greet the Other as a holy guest and urge its own residents to venture out to engage with the world. This is the way of progressive faith: An open door stands at the threshold of our theological house, its doorsill well-worn by comings and goings.

Every September, on the day after Labor Day, the faculty, staff, and I gather on the front porch of Starr King School for the Ministry and invite the entering class to cross the school's threshold together. Fall is just beginning to tinge the air. The sycamores that line the street have become a mottled mix of green and gold. The sun gleams through their leaves, creating a diaphanous canopy sheltering the new seminarians who stand before the door, ready to begin. Fresh scrubbed and dressed in new clothes, they look excited and dazed. It is the first day of school, and something about that is the same whether it's kindergarten or graduate school. They are many ages—from young people just out of college to elders who have completed a long career in law or medicine and now want to dedicate themselves to religious service. Like our faculty and staff, the students are diverse ethnically, culturally, and religiously. Among them are liberal Christians, practicing Buddhists, devoted Unitarian Universalists, Hindus, Muslims, pagans, religious humanists, Jews—and combinations of the above.

Each of them is on a mission: a mission to go deeper in their religious understanding and practice; a mission to be of greater service to the common good; a mission to be more faithful to their own heart and more helpful to their communities. Some are responding to a calling they have felt since childhood but held just as a dream. Others are startled to find themselves at this threshold, having uprooted their whole lives to take a path whose destination is unclear. I greet them and invite them to come together through the school's open door.

The drummers begin to beat out a rhythm. The singers start a simple refrain, and voices join in singing words of Rūmī: "Come, come whoever you are, wanderer, worshipper, lover of leaving, ours is no caravan of despair." Colorful prayer flags float in the breeze, strung between the lintel posts. As the new students cross the threshold, some reach out their hand to touch the mezuzah on the doorpost or lean to kiss it. Its scroll in Hebrew instructs: "You shall love God with all your heart, with all your soul, with all your mind, and with all your strength." Others take off their shoes and enter barefoot. Soon everyone has assembled in the Fireside Room, which doubles as the school's chapel. Its roof beams are adorned with symbols from all the world's religions.

A sense of religious mission is not easy to live with. It can lead people to places they never expected to go and ask things of them that they are unsure they can do; they can be driven by a force beyond themselves to which they have surrendered. People are often wary of those who are "on a mission from God." Sometimes the spirit that drives them is overbearing, dominating, or even demonic. Liberals and progressives have been rightly skeptical of religious zeal—especially missionary zeal when it seeks to impose its will and its way on others and has uncritically imposed cultural dominance, or supported colonizing agendas, in the name of God.

When I began as a young parish minister, I was determined to avoid any kind of proselytizing or evangelism. I didn't assume that my liberal Christian commitments were something that anybody *else* should be committed to; nor did I believe that Christianity had an exclusive claim on the truth. I preferred to live and let live. But then I was assigned by my bishop to a congregation on the verge of closing. The active membership was down to about fifty people, many of them in their eighties. They had spent their whole lives in together in their church, loving one another and the place until it shined with a patina of care. It seemed to me such a place should not close its doors. But it wasn't going to remain open unless it attracted some new members.

I decided to keep my eyes open for any visitors that wandered into the church. Almost every Sunday, someone would show up. When they did, I'd visit them the following week, arriving unannounced at their doorway. Often they were surprised, but almost everyone was hospitable. They would invite me in, offer me a cup of coffee or tea, and we'd talk. People told me why they'd crossed the threshold into the church. No one, it turned out, ever dropped in casually, as if they'd awakened on Sunday morning with nothing appealing to do and found that reading the *New York Times* over coffee seemed boring that day.

People came to church for life-and-death reasons. Susan came because she'd just given birth to a baby after years of trying to get pregnant and suffering miscarriages. Her joy was great, and she was searching for a way to say thank you. She came to church to offer gratitude for life and to seek support in raising her child within a loving community. Thomas and Vince came when Thomas lost his job because the school district was firing gay teachers. He was heartbroken and angry, and they were worried about making ends meet. They were looking for some word of encouragement, an expression of kindness that might ease their pain and give them some hope. John came because he was depressed; he worked in the aerospace industry, and his job was to design computer systems that would allow a nuclear exchange to be carried on even if all U.S. military personnel had been killed. He hadn't become a scientist for this, but his family depended on him keeping his job. He came to the church because his values called him to something different, but he couldn't do it alone. Elizabeth and Rodrigo came because they'd fallen in love and decided to marry. They were looking for a sacred place and a sacred community to bless their union. Julia came because she'd just been diagnosed with cancer. She was frightened; her family was overwhelmed. Where would she find the spiritual strength she needed to endure chemotherapy? Elvira came because she was grieved and alarmed at the threats to world peace and ecological sustainability. She was working hard to bring about change, but she needed soul sustenance. She was searching for something deeper than anger to keep her going.

People crossed the threshold of our neighborhood church impelled by life's joys, injustices, difficulties, and hopes. They came looking for a way to amplify their happiness, solidify their commitments, ease their difficulties, and fulfill their hopes. They came believing that the church could do all these things. I responded by asking them to help rebuild our small congregation: to teach Sunday school, to serve on the social justice committee, to sing in the choir, to help us raise money for the United Methodist Committee on Relief and the General Board of Global Ministries. Nearly everyone I visited said yes. The church began to grow. Our sense of shared mission deepened, anchored in the longings of the heart that had brought each person there. And I changed my mind about "missions" and "evangelism." I recognized that what our church did, what it stood for, and why it existed mattered profoundly. It was humbling to see that we had gifts and resources that people truly needed. It behooved us to open our doors more proactively, to invite people in from the highways and byways. The progressive church holds a feast of life spread for all—it is ours to share with any who can find nourishment within our walls.

Some approach Christian evangelism with an exclusive claim that "this is the right way, and you are damned if you don't agree." Liberal and progressive religion does not require this stance. Our path is one among many. At the dawn of the twenty-first century, we can approach mission with an ecumenical and interfaith consciousness that appreciates religious diversity as a gift.

Passages from the Christian scriptures provide a foundation for Christians to let go of any exclusive claim to the truth. "My father's mansion has many rooms," Jesus says in John's Gospel, refuting those who would compel religious conformity. Liberals, for the past two centuries, have emphasized tolerance and generous openness to diversity in religious practice, ideas, and orientations. In I Corinthians 15, Paul speaks of diversity as a sign of God's life-giving creativity, reasoning that diverse forms in nature provide evidence for the Resurrection:

> The flesh of living beings is not all the same kind of flesh; human beings have one kind of flesh, animals another, birds another, and fish another. And there are heavenly bodies and earthly bodies; the beauty that belongs to heavenly bodies is different from the beauty that belongs to earthly bodies. The sun has its own beauty, the moon another beauty and the stars a different beauty, and even among the stars there are different kinds of beauty. This is how it will be when the dead are raised to life. What is sown is perishable, what is raised is imperishable....It is sown a physical body, it is raised a spiritual body.

For Christians, ecumenical and interfaith engagement can be grounded in this understanding of the Resurrection: life is filled with changing bodies of diverse, wondrous kinds, each with its own distinctive beauty. The Creator of life creates multiple forms, and these are a sign of God's resurrecting power.

The world's various religious traditions can be respected as manifestations of God's life-giving spirit that creates splendid diversity—not uniformity.

Twenty-first-century ecumenism must embrace the distinctive and multiple forms of beauty in which Christians of different ethnicities, histories, theologies, and cultures embody their relationship to Christ, and witness to the life-giving activity of God with us in spirit and in truth. There is no need whatsoever to create one Christian culture, one worship practice, or even one doctrine. Nor need Christians stay isolated in separate communions—we can participate in one another's ways of worship—and discover ourselves more richly joined to Christ *because of* rather than *despite* the multiple forms. For pluralism is a sign of God's creativity, a sign of life, a sign of resurrection.

This affirmation of diversity can extend beyond Christian ecumenism to multireligious life and learning. Multireligious community fosters openness to the diversities of beauty that can be found within the rich and complex forms of religious cultures on the globe. Life is vibrant in plenitude, in variety, in particularity, and in local embodiments. Humanity's religious diversity, in short, gives glory to God, and the ecumenism and interfaith awareness of the twenty-first century will not only tolerate or accept diversity. It will reverence it as a sign of God's life-giving presence in the world. It will seek to preserve cultural distinctiveness while also enhancing our experiences of hospitality and exchange among one another's places and ways of being religious. I have learned from my Muslim colleagues and friends that God's revelation to Mohammed points this way as well. The Qur'an states:

Humankind, We have created you male and female, and appointed you races and tribes, that you may know one another.

Progressive faith offers a wide welcome for those who come to its door. It has hope to offer, and it gives people room to breathe. Its theological boundaries make a life-giving, affirming faith possible—providing a defining structure of meaning. Its message is worth proclaiming openly and broadly.

Within the theological house of progressive faith there is room for tremendous variety, diversity, and dissent. But there is also a defining focus: a devotion to the flourishing of life. People of progressive faith care for the sacredness of this world, this life, here and now. We do not look to a world to come that will be more valuable than this world. We cherish our bodies, this earth, this time and place that is within our grasp. We reverence the intimate, intricate, and unshakeable reality that all life is connected. We honor and respect the bonds that tie each to all, that weave us into an inescapable net of mutuality. We vow to care for the interdependent web of existence; we desire all life to thrive, and therefore we resist those social evils and systemic injustices that benefit a few at the expense of many, or that allow a privileged existence for some while others have their hearts and bodies broken by exploitation, prejudice, censure, or lack of access to the rights and resources needed for life. We critique any conception of God that functions to bless an unjust status quo or to alleviate human responsibility. We affirm a covenant among all beings that we honor with our hearts, souls, mind, and strength. We will do everything in our power to assure that this covenant of life, for life, is honored. And we seek to connect our circle with other circles of life, to expand our circle into ever-widening ripples of influence for good.

Expanding the circles of people "united together for life" is the mission of progressive faith. This mission matters in a world threatened by violence, injustice, and ecological exploitation. For Christians, Jesus's prayer in John's Gospel, "May they be one," is a touchstone text. This prayer for oneness—for faithful connectedness one to another and to God—is offered by Jesus in the presence of a grave threat. The threat was not differences in worship styles, or arguments about fine points of theological doctrine. Jesus was not praying that everyone would think alike or worship in the same way. He and the disciples faced the Roman Empire's divide-and-conquer tactics. They led an oppressed people who were struggling for survival, and many of them were crucified by Rome for doing so. The Gospels predict fragmentation of Jesus's disciples as the likely outcome of the violence against Jesus. "The shepherd is struck and the sheep will be scattered." Jesus prays that this will not be so—that the forces of an unjust empire will not also break apart his disciples. If we contemplate Jesus's prayer for the unity of his disciples in the context of his imminent betrayal into the hands of his enemies, we can see that this prayer encourages humanity to confront together, without being torn asunder, the principalities and powers that continue to crucify the sacred ones of God.

The crucifying powers remain active in the world. Liberal theologian Walter Rauschenbusch named these forces militarism, religious bigotry, mob-spirit, greed and economic exploitation, and corruption of justice systems. These are the sins, he said, that killed Jesus. Unity resists. It forges a faithfulness to one another and to the holy that enables people to hold fast to love for life and for one another. United, people stand fast in the presence of the systemic evils that crucify life. How can we find such unity? What can bind us together as people of diverse faiths to stand together on behalf of life, and in resistance to the destructive practices that threaten earth's people and the earth itself?

Shared acts of compassion and justice-making create unity. People forge unity with one another by working together to respond to the abuses of empire, economic inequity, ecological exploitation, militarism, and the ongoing evils of racism, sexism, and heterosexism that fragment life. These abuses break the solidarity of humanity and the intimacy of connection between humanity and the earth; these powers crucify God's people and threaten the earth. When people engage in resisting these powers, unity grows. This is why we must engage in an ecumenics of solidarity. But the question remains, how can we find such unity when the very nature of these forces is to tear us apart and when some forms of religion are aligned with these crucifying forces?

We also need an ecumenics of beauty. We need a shared reverence for the goodness of this earth, our lives, our cultures and communities—an ecumenics of praise and gratitude, appreciation, and respect. The ecumenical and multireligious mission of progressive faith is to strengthen solidarity by holding fast to what is good, what protects and saves life, in the presence of crucifying powers that threaten earth and earth's people.

The mission of progressive faith is to embrace the beauty of diversity and the diversity of beauty; to resist the crucifying powers by ministries of solidarity; to love one another and this earth as paradise, here and now, the place Jesus promised us we would be when he said, "Today you will be with me in paradise."

This mission requires each person to answer the question, What will you do with your gifts? And it requires vibrant commitment to life together in community. The words with which I greet each new class of seminarians at Starr King at the front door on the first day of school form a fitting invitation to any and all who want to join this caravan of joy:

We are here at the threshold.
We are here,

We who have crossed many thresholds already
to arrive at this space and time,
Coming out—from identities and locations that

didn't embrace the fullness of who we are;
Coming across—distances, boundaries,
discoveries that have beckoned us to deeper life
and challenged us to change;
Coming with—our loves, our partners, our children,
our memories, our knowledge,
our wisdom, and our willingness;
Coming to—our senses, our awareness
of the critical issues that threaten the well-being
of earth's creatures, communities, and cultures;
Coming again—to decisions, commitments, hopes,
determinations that we know matter.
We are *here* at this threshold,
the threshold of a house of study,
where minds and hearts are on fire;
the threshold of a house of spirit
where prayer and contemplation
take us deeper;
the threshold of a house of hope
for greater justice and compassion in the world;
the threshold of a house of history
that can inform our present lives
and link us to a communion that
crosses the boundary of death;
the threshold of a house of preparation
for the thresholds we will lead others to cross,
for the thresholds yet to come,
for the thresholds the world stands on—
poised, now, as always
between the possibilities of violence
and the possibilities of peace.
Come, let us cross this threshold
together.

CHAPTER THIRTEEN

A Call to Partnership

John Buehrens

"The church exists by mission the way a fire exists by burning," said theologian Emil Brunner. And when the worship is over, then the service begins. But does liberal and progressive religion really know its mission? How is that mission to be understood?

The late Wallace Robbins, who served as dean of Rockefeller Chapel at the University of Chicago, often said that "the mission of liberal religion is to make religion more liberal and to make liberals more religious." I can agree, even now substituting the term "progressive." But I also want to deepen that rather-too-clever formulation.

Evangelicals know that their mission is chiefly to spread the gospel. Progressive evangelicals, however, along with liberal Christians, add that this is best done not just by talking about Jesus, but also by helping to realize the kingdom, the commonwealth of God that he proclaimed. This means living the religion of Jesus, in his prophetic spirit, by performing the *mitzvot* of feeding the hungry, clothing the naked, healing

the sick, proclaiming liberty to the oppressed, and saying that
now is the acceptable time for justice, healing, and reconcilia-
tion. As Francis of Assisi is said to have put it, "Preach the
gospel always; when necessary, use words."

Those of us who are heirs of the Enlightenment in religious
thinking have an additional mission in the twenty-first century,
however. It is time for us to stop thinking that we have the bur-
den of bringing enlightenment to other cultures. Rather our
mission now is to partner with others who are different from
us and to learn from them about the path to creating a more
hopeful and life-giving world for all of earth's peoples.

Never did I learn more about this side of our mission than
when I went to India in February of 2001, after the devastating
earthquake in the state of Gujarat destroyed more than a million homes. Arriving at the airport in Mumbai, I was met by
my friend Vivek Pandit. He and his wife won global recognition in 1999 from Antislavery International for their work in
freeing more than fifteen thousand tribal people in the hills
above Mumbai from modern slavery, or "bonded labor." As we
embraced and waited for my bags, we found ourselves gradually
surrounded by a growing crowd of people both curious and
increasingly hostile.

"Is he a missionary?" some were asking, pointing at me.
They were Hindu nationalists. Their party was in power. Fired
by postcolonial claims to cultural self-determination (and too
often playing off prejudice against both Muslims and lower-
caste converts to Christianity), they were saying that if I was
a missionary, I should be put back on a plane and sent away.
They'd had too much experience of Western missionaries con-
tributing to the economic and cultural subjugation of their
people.

"Yes!" Vivek began to shout. (This was all translated for
me later.) "Yes! He *is* a missionary! But you have not asked

what his mission is! His mission is human rights—not changing anyone's religion! His mission is homes for the homeless of Gujarat! Freedom for bonded laborers! Human dignity for all! Now—what is your mission? Fear? Hatred? How unworthy! Go away yourselves!" And before what Gandhi might have called the *satyagraha*, the truth force in Vivek's courageous soul, the menacing crowd simply dispersed.

I was in India for several reasons. My own religious community has several kinds of partners in mission there. Some are human rights workers like Vivek. One of our programs has formed a partnership with him and his labor union of former bonded laborers. Together, through an amazing network of grass-roots activists, our partners work to empower India's women, *dalits* (untouchables), *adivasi* (indigenous) groups, and others who have been oppressed or marginalized. All of us covenant to counter any attempt at turning one religious or ethnic identity against another and to learn from one another.

I was also there to visit some indigenous Unitarians, in the far Khasi Hills of northeast India. Their history illustrates the creative way people who have been colonized can sometimes turn tables on their colonizers. Before the British came in the 1850s with their soldiers, traders, and missionaries, the Khasis practiced their own ancient, tribal religion—quite unrelated to Hinduism. The British set out to convert the whole region to Christianity, setting up mission schools. One of the first graduates of the secondary program was a brilliant young man named Hajom Kissor Singh. Asked to speak at his graduation, he said (in effect): "We Khasis should probably thank you British for introducing us to the spiritual and moral teaching of Jesus. After all, if nothing else, this tells us how you tell yourselves you *should* treat other human beings! Now, just a few questions: Why do you want us to believe things about him he never spoke about? Would it not be enough just to treat one another as all children of the one God he called Father, that others call Mother, that our Khasi tradition calls Blei [Spirit], that Hindus have so many names for, that the Muslims call Allah? Would that not be enough?"

The missionaries—hellfire-and-brimstone Calvinists from Wales—said he was a "heretic" of the worst kind, a kind they had back in Wales. Why, what he was saying made him a Unitarian! To which Hajom Kissor Singh replied, "Ah! Then I have something else to thank you for! It is never good to be all alone in life. Better to have spiritual partners. Unitarian? You have an address for them, maybe?"

Obviously I dramatize a bit. But the amazing thing to me about the Unitarian Union of Northeast India is that it is not the product of mission work; it is an indigenous movement that looked for partners. Hajom Kissor Singh found the first one in the person of the Reverend Charles H. A. Dall, an American Unitarian minister then working in Calcutta at a pioneering school for girls. Dall had been one of my predecessors in Needham, serving First Parish from 1847 to 1850. Earlier he'd been a Unitarian missionary to the urban poor in St. Louis, Baltimore, and Portsmouth, New Hampshire. But in each place the privileged Unitarian patrons of his efforts failed to follow through on the implications of what partnership with the poor might require of them. He took the semirural pulpit in Needham out of some desperation. He and his brilliant wife, Caroline Healey Dall, had started a family. While they lived in Needham, they had a child who died shortly after birth. Charles Dall failed at the ministry in Needham and, after that, in Toronto. One day he came home to tell Caroline that he had accepted a "mission post" teaching in Calcutta. She and their children stayed in Boston. They never divorced. But he visited home only three times before he died in India in 1886.

By that time Dall had helped Hajom Kissor Singh trans-

late into Khasi materials for a worship book. It included ex-
cerpts from the prophets and Jesus, but also from Channing,
Emerson, Unitarian prayers and hymns, and many that Singh
himself wrote to the One God, Blei. There are now nearly ten
thousand members in more than thirty-five Khasi congregations in the Unitarian Union of Northeast India. Most are
subsistence farmers. But when I spoke to them at their annual
gathering about the Gujarat earthquake and about our efforts
with the Self-Employed Women's Association to help the most
vulnerable rebuild their lives, they took up a collection to help
out. They presented me with a plastic sack of rupee notes almost six feet in diameter! The leaders spent the night changing
rupee notes into larger bills for me to carry with me.

Progressive religious people today must put a shared sense
of mission into partnerships that are not paternalistic, but
egalitarian; they must cross boundaries of culture and class to
unite diverse groups in shared work for a greater good. I can
illustrate this closer to home as well. Currently my congregation has a partnership with an inner-city school—not to pros-
elytize there, of course, but simply to help and to learn. Our
volunteers work with children of immigrants who have no one
at home to help with English. The volunteers help staff an
after-school program for children whose parents must be at
work then. This partnership is not one-way, however. It also
helps people from the suburbs to learn about the realities and
life struggles of children in a school that has far fewer resources
than the ones in Needham. As immigrant children gain some
multicultural skills that they will need to survive and thrive in a
dominant culture different from their own, suburban volunteers
learn that although the earth may be increasingly "flat" because
of globalization, the playing field is often terribly tilted. My
congregation also partners with a village in eastern Uganda
through a nongovernmental organization, African Baobab, cre-

ated by two of our most outreaching parishioners. It helps an area with many children who have been orphaned by AIDS.

Nor does it stop there. We also partner with a regional shelter for homeless families, helping families prepare to move back to more stable situations, and learning about the need for transitional and affordable housing. We have a team in an interfaith partnership called Partakers, partnering with prisoners trying to earn a college degree while incarcerated, and learning about the expensive, self-defeating aspects of a penal system that is almost entirely punitive rather than rehabilitative.

In our partnerships, at times it can feel as if all we are doing is trying to hold back an ever-rising tide of short-sightedness, neglect, exploitation, oppression, and disease. But when that overwhelms me, I try to recall another experience that I had with our partners in India.

In the hills above Mumbai there is place called Usgaon that was developed by Vivek and his union of bonded laborers, with help from partners, into a training center for activists. It always reminds me of the Highlander Center outside Knoxville, Tennessee, where Rosa Parks decided, after a workshop, not to sit in the back of the bus any longer; where Dr. King both learned and taught nonviolent confrontation with injustice; where Guy Carawan, the music director of Highlander, once changed a song. He had been out listening to and collecting songs of the Gullah-speaking descendants of slaves on the Georgia Sea Islands. One had become a hymn. Evangelicals called it, "I Shall Overcome." Guy heard it and, with Zilphia Horton, wife of Highlander's founder, Myles Horton, transformed it into the anthem we now know as "We Shall Overcome." Pete Seeger and others spread it.

The first time I met in India with all the "struggle partners" who support Usgaon, they ended a day of reflecting on how they could better learn from and support one another with an evening of singing. They came from every caste and from no caste; from every religion of India and from no religion; from many of the seventeen major language groups, and from several of the hundreds of less widely known ones. All these creative activists for human rights and justice were brought together by an amazing woman named Kathy Sreedhar. American and Jewish by birth, Kathy is the widow of a progressive Indian economist. She is also mentor, facilitator, and "Jewish mother" to this network of activists in India.

They began with what they call "struggle songs"—expressions of the human spirit longing for justice, many like the African American songs that crossed the color line in the American civil rights movement. As the time came to close, they said, "Now, Kathy and John, we want to sing one that you can join in on." Although the words were strange at first— Vivek kept identifying the languages: Hindi, Gujarati, Bengali, Tamil, several others—we both recognized the simple melody. Finally, for us, they ended in English. I joined my partners in singing the familiar words, "We Shall Overcome."

Sometimes when I had sung that song the words had rung hollow. Not this time. This time I remembered that enslaved people brought that melody with them from Africa. Civil rights activists that I had known personally had turned it from a personal prayer for endurance into an anthem of collective resistance. It was one that inspired the whole generation in America in which I came of age, making us more determined never to give up—not in the face of fire hoses, billy clubs, jailings, bombings, assassinations; dangers that my partners in India knew all too well. Now I was hearing that same "struggle song"—one brought halfway around the globe and sung back to me by people with whom I share a hope and a mission. Tears rolled down my cheeks as I sang, grateful to have received back from partners the determination of a hope that I needed not to lose.

To be progressive in religion means to hold on to that hope, to recognize the mission that is inspired by it, and to embrace that mission in partnership with others, bringing all the strength of our diverse cultures, languages, and creeds together to serve justice.

Back home, in the old meetinghouse in Needham where I preach most Sundays, there is one dimension of the architecture that I have not mentioned as yet. Our church also has a steeple, with a bell in the tower. It's a bell cast by the foundry of Paul Revere. It was hung there two hundred years ago, when our nation was young and revolutionary. Its purpose was then—as it remains now—to summon the people. We ring it at the start of every service. We ring it in times of public emergency. We call people to partner with us in serious discussions about the common good and the human future.

Let this little book now end with the sound of that bell. Coauthors though Rebecca and I are, we may not agree in all aspects of the progressive theology described herein. That is quite fine with both us. The two of us have enjoyed a long dialogue that's helped to deepen our lives. We live in different regions of this great continent. Our backgrounds and experience differ. So do yours. If democracy, justice, and peace are to prevail, then a global Town Meeting is in order. Let it begin in the spirit not of sectarianism, but rather of progressive religion, in all of its dimensions.

Come to the global meetinghouse! Sing the songs of others. Hear them sing yours back to you until you yourself are changed. Be a partner in hope. And, wherever you live, help to make yours a house of hope for others. One where all who speak may feel they are heard, and where the voice that issues forth is one not of despair for this world's ills, but of hope for a shared future.

Now hear the bell ring! And then pray, and then sing!

ACKNOWLEDGMENTS

We thank the Liberal Religious Educators Association for the invitation to Rebecca Parker that led to this book. Dialogue with students at Andover Newton Theological School, Harvard Divinity School, and Starr King School for the Ministry has stimulated and inspired our thinking, as has conversation with faculty, congregants, and colleagues both ordained and lay. The late Patti Lawrence, professor of congregational studies at SKSM, is especially remembered, with great affection, for her sustained practical wisdom with regard to the development of effective, progressive religious communities, and for her enthusiasm for lifelong theological learning. We are grateful for those whose personal life stories are included in this book—we have learned much from each of them: especially Amy Moses-Lagos, Megan Ernst Wittenberg, and the late Joan Valdina.

A grant from the Fund for Unitarian Universalism supported our collaborative research and writing. Both the First Parish in Needham and Starr King School for the Ministry provided institutional support and periods of professional leave devoted to the project. At Beacon Press the leadership of Helene Atwan and the editorial skill of Amy Caldwell offered steady encouragement, patience, and important critical guidance.

Finally, we are most deeply indebted to our families—to those who raised us and gave us the freedom to think critically and serve faithfully, and to those who are our partners in life, Joanne M. Braxton and Gwen Langdoc Buehrens, devoted, respectively, to the liberatory practice of writing and teaching, and to the art of authentic ministry. We thank them for their forbearance and their love.